The Andy Guide to

WINDOWS® 10

Andrew Warren

The Scribbler (DOTBIZ) Ltd

Published by The Scribbler (DOTBIZ) Limited

Copyright © Andrew J. Warren, 2015

Andrew J. Warren asserts his rights under the Copyright, Designs and Patents Act, 1988 to be identified as the author of this work.

This book is sold subject to the condition that it shall not, by way of trade or otherwise, be lent, resold, hired out, or otherwise circulated without the publisher's prior consent in any form of binding or cover other than that in which it is published and without a similar condition including this condition being imposed on the subsequent publisher.

First published in the United Kingdom in 2015 by The Scribbler (DOTBIZ) Limited, 88 Edgware Way, Edgware, Middlesex, HA8 8JS, UK.

All trademarks are gratefully acknowledged and are the property of the respective owners.

All rights reserved. No parts of this book may be reproduced, in any form or by any means, without written permission from the publisher.

www.thescribbler.biz

Contents

CONTENTS 1
INTRODUCTION 4
ABOUT THE AUTHOR 4
PREFACE 5
CHAPTER 1 7
INTRODUCING WINDOWS 10 7
WHAT'S NEW IN WINDOWS 10? 8
   New since Windows 7 and earlier *9*
   New since Windows 8.1 .... *11*
SELECTING A WINDOWS 10 EDITION 13
   Choosing an appropriate device *13*
   Windows 10 Editions *15*
   32-bit or 64-bit? *18*
CAN I UPGRADE TO WINDOWS 10? 19
CHAPTER 2 21
NAVIGATING THE INTERFACE 21
NAVIGATING WITH TOUCH 22
   Signing in *22*
   Accessing Start *24*
   Customizing Start *25*
   Accessing Settings *29*
NAVIGATING WITH A MOUSE AND KEYBOARD 31
   Signing in *31*
   Accessing Start *31*
   Customizing Start *31*
   Accessing Settings *31*
USING SHORTCUT KEYS 32
CHAPTER 3 33
CONNECTING TO THE INTERNET 33
MANAGING NETWORK CONNECTIONS 34
   Things you need before you start *34*
   Establishing a wireless connection *34*
   Managing your wireless connection *38*
USING A MICROSOFT ACCOUNT 39
   What is a Microsoft account? *39*
   Creating a Microsoft account *39*

Introduction - Contents

Using OneDrive 45
    What is OneDrive? *45*
Synchronizing Settings 49

CHAPTER 4 51

CUSTOMIZING WINDOWS 51

Personalizing Your Device 52
    Choosing a theme *52*
    Choosing a colour scheme *54*
    Configuring Lock screen options *55*
    Configuring Start options *58*
Configuring Display Settings 59
Tablet Mode 63
Action Centre 66
    Determining what you are notified about *68*

CHAPTER 5 71

WORKING WITH APPS 71

Configuring Mail, People, and Calendar 72
    Configuring Mail *73*
    Configuring Calendar *79*
    Configuring People *81*
Installing Windows Store Apps 82
    Installing an app *82*
    Managing your apps *84*
Installing Desktop Apps 91
    32-bit or 64-bit *91*
    Installing Office 2013 .... *91*
    User Account Control *98*
Switching Between Apps 100

CHAPTER 6 103

SECURITY 103

Configuring Windows Firewall 104
    What is a firewall? *104*
    Windows Firewall *104*
Using Windows Defender 109
    What is malicious software? *109*
    Windows Defender *109*
Implementing BitLocker 114
    The importance of drive encryption *114*
    Enabling BitLocker *115*
    Using BitLocker drives *118*
    Manage BitLocker *119*

Introduction - Contents

CHAPTER 7 121

CONNECTING PERIPHERALS 121

CONNECTING PRINTERS 122
   Initial setup *122*
   Managing a Printer *128*
CONFIGURING BLUETOOTH 131
   Preparing to use Bluetooth *131*
   Connecting a Bluetooth peripheral *133*
MANAGING STORAGE DEVICES 137
   Adding a storage card *138*

CHAPTER 8 145

TROUBLESHOOTING AND RECOVERY 145

WINDOWS UPDATE 146
   Configuring Windows Update *146*
THE IMPORTANCE OF BACKUP 150
   Using Backup and Restore (Windows 7) *150*
   Using File History *154*
   Using Previous Versions to restore files *157*
RECOVERY OPTIONS IN WINDOWS 10 160
   Creating restore points with System Protection *161*
   Using a restore point to revert to a previous system configuration *163*
   Using Advanced Startup *166*
   Recovery partitions *170*

CONGRATULATIONS 171

THIS IS THE END OF THE BOOK 171

Introduction

About the author

Andy has worked in the Information Technology business for almost 30 years. In 1988, he joined the US networking and software company, 3Com, as a system engineer. He was responsible for assisting with the launch of their Microsoft® LAN Manager-based network operating system, 3+Open.

Since then, Andy has focused on Microsoft-based software and technologies. He is a Microsoft Certified Systems Engineer, a Microsoft Certified Trainer, and a CompTIA CTT+ trainer. He has taught hundreds of classes to thousands of students over the years. In the last decade, Andy has been involved in designing and developing courseware for Microsoft Learning in Redmond.

Aside from technology, Andy has a great interest in military history and has written four novels about the First World War.

He lives in rural Somerset in the UK with his wife and daughter.

Preface

Microsoft® Windows® has been with us for several decades, first shipping back in the 1980s as a replacement for the text-based operating system, DOS. Major technical updates have come every couple of years. Sometimes, these technical updates are accompanied by significant user interface changes.

Microsoft might be the first to admit that these changes to their flagship operating system haven't always been well received. Windows 2000® was vastly superior to the Windows 98® series it replaced, being based in the Windows NT® engine. However, the uptake outside of corporate organizations was disappointing. Windows XP®, with a redesigned look, was very successful, and even now, when official support is no longer available for this platform, it is still widely used. Windows Vista™, its replacement, never did well despite being little different, architecturally, from its popular successor, Windows 7.

Some argue that Microsoft tried to do too much too soon with Windows 8 and Windows 8.1, attempting to shoehorn into Windows support for multiple devices (touch and non-touch) and multiple app platforms (traditional desktop apps, such as Microsoft Office®, and Windows Store-based apps designed for the Modern UI). The result was, perhaps, confusion.

Windows 10 seeks to address these issues. Microsoft provides the same interface and the same app store for a variety of device types: phones, tablets, laptops, and even desktop computers. The interface works equally well for touch and also non-touch devices. Learn to use Windows 10 on your Microsoft Surface™ tablet, and you should have no problem using it on your Nokia phone. And your apps and settings will move with you between your devices.

Microsoft have learned that infrequent, big step changes in their update cycle, such as from Windows XP to Windows Vista, are unpopular – and for large organizations, expensive. Windows 10 will be the last such major, single update. From now on, smaller updates will be released more frequently, and they will be handled by the Windows Update service just as patches and fixes are handled now.

So, for those of you with a new device, or those of you thinking of upgrading an earlier version of Windows to Windows 10 (initially, for free), what's in it for you? This book seeks to answer that question, and provide you with the skills necessary to use, configure and maintain the latest client operating system from Microsoft, Windows 10.

Introduction - Preface

This page left intentionally blank

Chapter 1

Introducing Windows 10

What you will do in this chapter:

- Describe the new features in Windows 10
- Choose the right device and appropriate edition of Windows 10
- Determine the upgrade options available for your existing version of Windows

What's New in Windows 10?

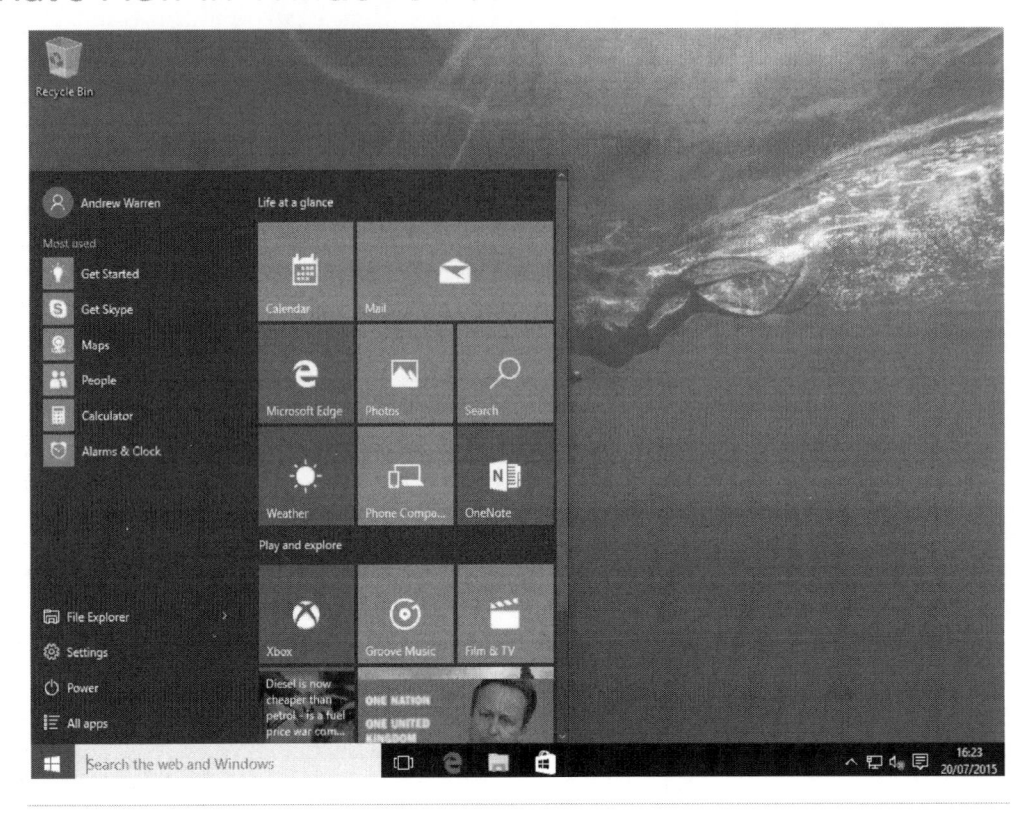

Figure 1.– The Windows 10 interface

Welcome to Windows 10!

What's new in Windows 10 depends largely on what your current operating system is. If you have a desktop computer installed with Windows XP, or even Windows 7, then you're in for a treat! The operating system is vastly improved over what you have. But if you're already using Windows 8.1, the changes are more nuanced, but still well worth a look.

Chapter 1 - Introducing Windows 10

New since Windows 7 and earlier

If you're a Windows 7 user, you'll notice the following differences when you switch to Windows 10.

- **Start screen**. This is the most obvious difference. Microsoft have created an alternative to the desktop (although the desktop is still present) to support tablet apps. As these apps require touch to work effectively, the desktop interface is not ideally suited. You can customize the Start screen to your own needs, adding, removing, and resizing tiles.

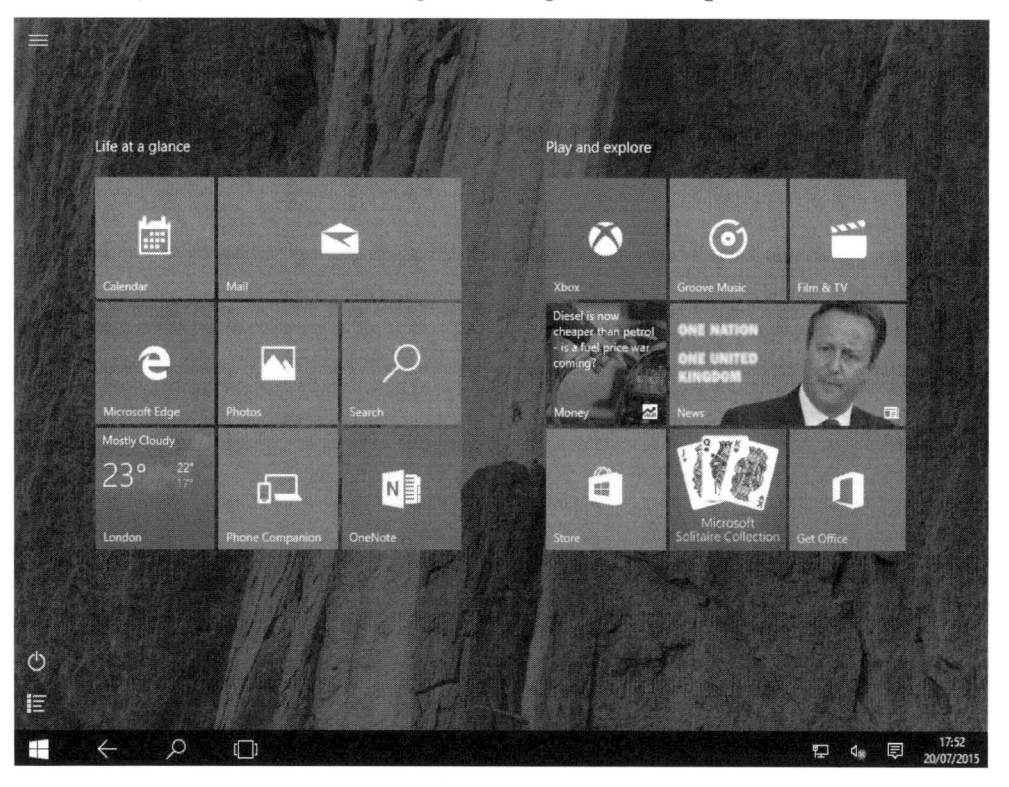

Figure 2.– Start screen

Chapter 1 - Introducing Windows 10

- **Recovery options**. Windows includes improved repair and recovery features. There was a time when if something went wrong with your computer, then you had no option but to return it to the store where you bought it and pay for someone to recover it. With Windows 10, there are more inbuilt recovery tools. Something goes wrong now, and you can probably fix it yourself if Windows doesn't manage to do it for you.

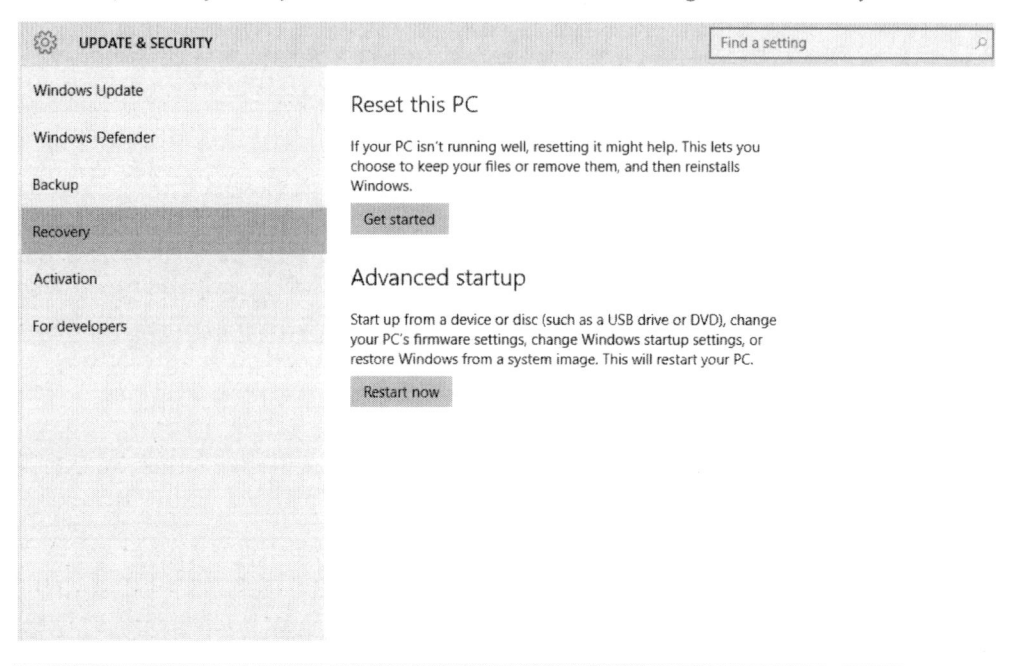

Figure 3.– Recovery options

- **Cloud**. When using apps, such as Microsoft Office, saving your files to the cloud is easier; Microsoft OneDrive® is always there as an option. This means when you save a Microsoft Office Word® document, or update a OneNote® file, if you switch devices, those files are available to you.

- **Bring your own device**. BYOD is an industry buzzword. Everyone's talking about how users can connect their own devices to their workplace network. Once upon a time, you went to work and you sat at a desk and you used the desktop computer provided by your employer. These days, people want to work from home, work on the road, hook up from customer sites. And they don't want to find that all their files are unavailable from these other locations, from these other devices. Windows provides features that enable you to easily connect your device to your workplace network: DirectAccess, Workplace Join, Work Folders, and Remote Desktop.

Note: Some of these BYOD features are only available on Windows 10 Enterprise edition.

New since Windows 8.1

Windows 8.1 users will see some significant improvements, including some great changes to the user interface based on user feedback on the Windows 8.1 platform.

- **Start**. There was much debate over the Windows 8 Start screen. Many corporate users felt that it got in the way of their desktop apps and bemoaned the loss of the Windows Start button. Microsoft addressed this to some extent in Windows 8.1 by bringing back a version of the Start button, and enabling Windows to sense whether it was loading on a tablet or laptop/desktop and choose the Start screen or desktop interface as appropriate. In Windows 10, this evolution continues, with the operating system sensing its environment and adapting accordingly. For desktop users, that is, users with a mouse, there is no Start screen, but rather a fully customizable Start button. For tablet users, the Start screen is even more touch aware.

- **Taskbar**. The thin bar at the bottom of the desktop is called the taskbar. In Windows 8, only desktop apps could be accessed from here. In Windows 10, any app – touch or desktop – can be found and controlled from the taskbar. This improved management of running apps extends to the whole interface. In Windows 8.1, Windows Store apps could only be accessed from the Start menu. Now, you can see them in resizable windows on the desktop, the same as any traditional desktop app.

Figure 4.– Taskbar

- **Universal apps**. In Windows 8, apps are available as apps for Windows 8, Windows 8 RT, or Windows 8 Phone edition. Windows 10 strives to eliminate that distinction. Apps will work on any platform. There is also a universal Windows Store from which both Windows Store apps and traditional desktop apps (like Microsoft Office) can be downloaded.

- **Cortana**. Microsoft introduced Cortana™ on some of its Windows Phone® devices last year. This voice assistant is now available across the range of Windows devices. Your own personal, digital assistant. You can use Cortana to search the web and content on your local Windows device. To activate Cortana, say *'Hey Cortana'*.

- **Multiple desktop**. If you have multiple monitors, its fairly easy to distribute your running apps across those displays. This is very useful if you want to

Chapter 1 - Introducing Windows 10

share your desktop during a video conference, for example, and want only to share certain apps. Windows 10 enables you to add multiple desktops even if you have only a single display. This enables you to separate apps into distinct virtual workspaces. To access this feature, click or touch the Task View icon on the taskbar and then touch New desktop.

- **Edge browser**. Not everyone was a fan of Internet Explorer™, with some claiming there were better browsers available, even for Windows. Microsoft has created an entirely new, cross-platform browser with a reading view (like the version in Windows Phone 8) and support for Cortana. It's lighter, faster, and more efficient.

Note: Internet Explorer 11 is still present in Windows 10. It may be required for certain websites or web-based apps that require specific ActiveX controls.

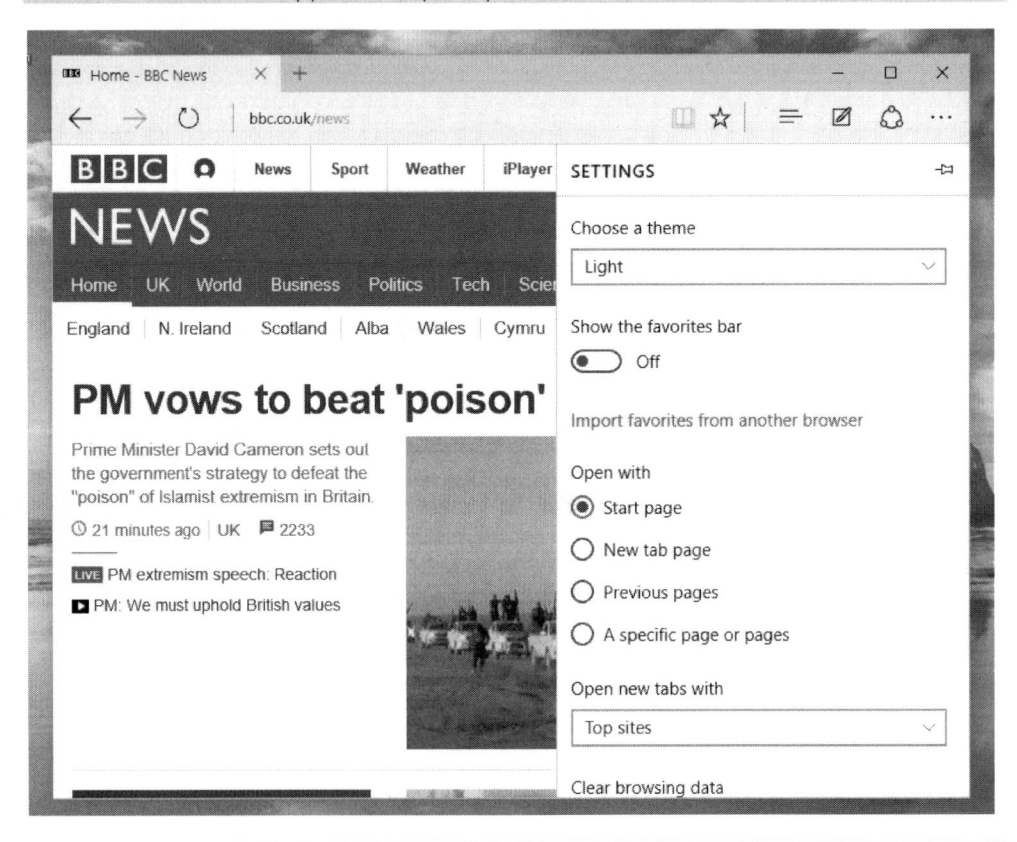

Figure 5.– Edge browser

Selecting a Windows 10 Edition

Choosing an appropriate device

Windows 10 is available on phones, tablets, laptops, and desktop computers. The device you choose depends on how you work, and perhaps where you work; clearly, using a desktop computer on the bus is a tricky and potentially unpopular proposition.

For many years, I have been searching for the perfect computing device; the one which combines the power of a desktop computer in the form factor of a small handheld device – but at the same time, accommodating my large fingers and weak eyes. Trust me, no such device exists – or is likely to in the near future.

So whatever device you choose must necessarily be a compromise; a balance between all your competing needs. If like me, you spend large amounts of time sitting in front of your device typing great volumes of text and working with graphical apps, then you're going to need something with a keyboard, a big high-resolution monitor, and possibly – probably, even – a mouse. Supplement this with a portable device, like a tablet or phone, for when you're out of the office.

If, however, you infrequently work on manuscripts, and have little need to manipulate graphics beyond posting to Facebook, then a tablet will work well for you. Many tablets even support the connection of external keyboards for those times when a touch keyboard just doesn't cut it.

Note: In fact, because Windows 10 supports Bluetooth, you can connect a Bluetooth keyboard to any device running Windows 10.

Windows 10 runs on the following device types.

- **Desktop computers**. A traditional computing device that gives very good performance but due to its size and shape is not very portable.
- **Laptops**. Nowadays, these seem to be the de facto computing platform offering a good balance between performance and portability. Generally, you can choose from a range of processor types and memory configurations depending on your needs and budget.
- **Convertibles**. These devices fall into one of two types: either they are primarily laptops with the ability to convert into a tablet by removing

elements, or they are first and foremost tablets to which you can add components to create a laptop. Using a tablet is a very different experience from using a laptop. This compromise device lets you do both – but as with all compromises, it can never do everything really well. That is, a convertible laptop is never as good as a pure laptop or a pure tablet being perhaps too small to be a laptop and too heavy to be a tablet.

- **Large tablets**. I am thinking of any tablet of around 11 inches or more. These devices give a good amount of screen space for your apps, but they are heavier and bulkier. They'll go into a shoulder bag, but not a pocket. They generally sport higher capacity batteries, but then due to their screen size, they require more power.

- **Small tablets**. Any device with a screen size of 8 inches or less falls into this category. These devices are great for consuming content: web browsing, viewing Office documents, reading books and magazines etc. But they're too small to work on for great lengths of time.

- **Phones**. Windows 10 is also available on Microsoft Phones. These range in size and performance from small devices for those with good eyes and small fingers, to large 'phablets' for those who want a hybrid capable of bridging the gap between phones and tablets. Many of these larger phones have 6 inch screens.

When planning to buy a Windows device, consider honestly what you want from it; what you're really going to do. Try to recognize that no one single device can do everything, and so you must balance your competing needs when you make your purchase.

If you want a portable device, but you must be able to work properly using it, then consider a convertible which is more laptop than tablet. If consuming content such as watching videos and playing music are what you want, then a phone or smaller tablet will be ideal. If you only use apps like email and Facebook, and occasionally type a letter or do your home finances in Microsoft Office Excel®, then you could probably use anything in the list – and your choice will probably come down to screen size.

Make sure you consider the following factors when you go to the store to buy your Windows 10 device.

- **Processor**. Although processors like the Intel® Core™ i7 run your apps fast, they consume more power, so you might find yourself having to be near an electrical socket to get any work done.

- **Screen**. Smaller is portable, but also harder to see. Some tablets now support very high resolutions even on fairly small devices. For instance, 1920 by 1080 is not uncommon even on 8 inch tablets. I would argue that at that resolution, on that screen size, text becomes very difficult to read.

- **Memory**. It is fairly unlikely that you can add memory after you buy your device (unless it's a desktop or laptop), so make sure you get a device with enough memory. For a tablet, especially the smaller sized devices, 2 GB is probably no problem. But for a laptop, you should be aiming for 8 GB minimum.

- **Storage and expansion options**. Most, if not all, of the Windows devices I have ever seen support standard expansion ports for the addition of storage cards. Micro SD ports, Micro USB, and USB ports are common, and you can add storage and swap storage as needed. My own Lenovo 8 inch tablet has a 64 GB storage card installed which I use to store my movies and music libraries.

- **Battery**. As with smartphones, so with Windows devices. The more you ask of it, and the higher the spec of the processor, the higher the screen resolution, the more the battery is drained. If being able to work without a charge is critical, research your device carefully and ensure that the battery has the required capacity.

Windows 10 Editions

Having chosen your device form factor, then you'll probably already have selected the edition of Windows 10. This is because new devices come pre-installed with an appropriate Windows edition. This was true for all preceding versions of Windows.

However, it is possible that on some devices, particularly high-end laptops and desktop computers, you may be able to select the edition when you order the device. If that's the case for you, which should you choose?

Chapter 1 - Introducing Windows 10

There are three main editions of Windows 10, all available in both 32-bit and 64-bit versions (see below).

- **Windows 10 Home**. Suitable for most home users, providing the main features that you need.

- **Windows 10 Pro**. Enables you to join your device to a work domain[1], and to use advanced features such as Boot from VHD, client Hyper-V, and BitLocker.

- **Windows 10 Enterprise**. As for Windows 10 Pro, but with the added capability to use AppLocker, Windows to Go[2], and DirectAccess[3], amongst other advanced features.

Note: In addition to the preceding editions of Windows 10, Windows 10 Mobile and Windows 10 Mobile Enterprise is available to customers that have a volume licensing arrangement with Microsoft. These editions are designed for use on small tablets and smartphones and come with a touch edition of Microsoft Office.

The following table provides guidance on the main features of each Windows 10 edition.

Feature	Windows 10 Home	Windows 10 Pro	Windows 10 Enterprise
Number of CPUs supported	1	2	2
Minimum memory	1 Gigabyte (GB) for 32-bit versions 2 GB for 64-bit versions	1 GB for 32-bit versions 2 GB for 64-bit versions	1 GB for 32-bit versions 2 GB for 64-bit versions
Maximum addressable memory[4]	128 GB	512 GB	512 GB
Workplace Join	Yes	Yes	Yes

[1] *A domain is a collection of computer devices managed by a single administrator and controlled by centralised policies.*

[2] *Windows to Go enables you to startup your device from a removable storage device such as a memory stick. The storage device has a complete Windows installation on it.*

[3] *DirectAccess is a remote connection technology used in large networks to enable users to work securely from almost anywhere.*

[4] *Memory is the working capacity of the device and determines how many apps you can run simultaneously and, to some extent, how fast the apps will run; this is analogous to the engine size of a car. Storage is how much content you can save to your device and is not limited by the operating system. Storage is analogous to the capacity of your car's boot (trunk).*

Chapter 1 - Introducing Windows 10

Feature	Windows 10 Home	Windows 10 Pro	Windows 10 Enterprise
Domain Join		Yes	Yes
Boot from VHD		Yes	Yes
BitLocker		Yes	Yes
AppLocker			Yes
Client Hyper-V		Yes (64-bit only)	Yes (64-bit only)
Windows to Go			Yes
DirectAccess			Yes

Figure 6.– Windows 10 Editions

Note: This table does not list all features for all editions.

Unless you specifically need a feature available in a different edition of Windows 10, use the edition that comes with your device.

32-bit or 64-bit?

For most users, whether the operating system is 32-bit or 64-bit is probably of little consequence. It's true that a number of features are only available in 64-bit variants of Windows 10. It's also true that in a high-end computer with lots of memory and fast, multicore processors, apps run much faster in 64-bit. But the truth is, your new Windows 10 device will almost certainly come with the appropriate version installed, so you don't need to worry overly about this.

That said, if you're interested, Windows 10 editions are all available in both 32-bit and 64-bit versions. Typically, your device will use a 64-bit version of Windows 10 as most hardware devices use 64-bit processors. Some devices, usually entry-level tablets, are installed with a 32-bit version of Windows 10.

64-bit operating systems support the ability to address more memory and to manage installed memory more effectively. This means that your apps will run better and probably faster, too. However, you will only notice a difference between 32-bit and 64-bit when you have more than 4 GB of memory installed as this is the maximum addressable by a 32-bit operating system.

Note: Actually, a 32-bit version of Windows addresses slightly less than 4 GB.

64-bit versions of Windows 10 also support a feature called Client Hyper-V. This feature enables you to create and use virtual machines. For most people, this is an irrelevance, and is only really useful if you want to run a legacy app that is designed to work on an earlier version of Windows, or on some other operating system entirely (such as Linux). A virtual machine creates a 'virtual' environment in which your legacy app runs.

Can I Upgrade to Windows 10?

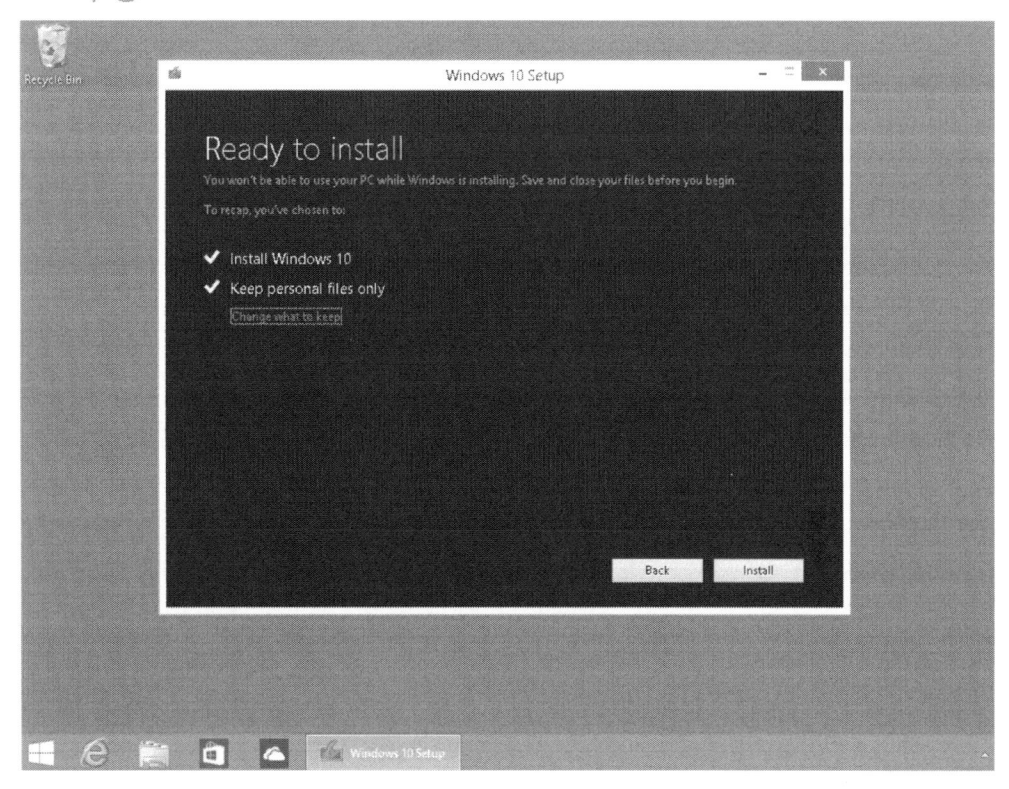

Figure 7.– Upgrading to Windows 10

Upgrading can be complex. You must determine whether your existing device is capable of running Windows 10. You must figure out whether you have enough free storage space to perform the upgrade. Finally, you will have to steel yourself for the process of overwriting the existing operating system with a new one, knowing that you almost certainly cannot revert this operation, and so if you mess it up, you'll have nothing.

Ultimately, I would recommend that most users simply replace their existing computer with a new Windows 10 device. But let me clarify that.

- If you are currently running Windows 7 on a computer that's three years old or more, it almost certainly won't have a touch screen. So, why upgrade to a touch-centric operating system? Just leave it alone and buy yourself a new device when you're ready.

- However, if you're currently running Windows 8 or 8.1 on a one or two year old laptop, then you can certainly consider replacing the operating

Chapter 1 - Introducing Windows 10

system with Windows 10. The good news is, the process for upgrading from Windows 8.1 is pretty easy.

This book is not the right place to provide detailed steps on upgrading your device to Windows 10 as there are too many variables and unknowns for me to give you accurate and relevant advice. However, if you are fairly technically minded, the following steps should provide you with sufficient guidance to have a go.

1. Make sure your computer is started and you are signed in with your Microsoft account[5].

2. Obtain the **Windows 10 product DVD**, or download the upgrade from the Windows Store[6].

Note: In order to ensure a smooth upgrade that retains your apps and settings, you must upgrade from and to supported editions. That is, upgrading from Windows 7 Home to Windows 10 Home results in you being able to retain both your apps and settings.

3. If the DVD does not autorun, double-click the DVD drive in **File Explorer**.

4. In the **License terms** window, select **I accept the license terms** and then touch **Accept**. Windows 10 setup now checks for updates (assuming you are connected to the Internet).

5. At the **Choose what to keep** page, choose whether to perform a clean installation[7] or an upgrade.

Note: The options you have here will depend on the specific edition of Windows you are upgrading from and to. For instance, when upgrading from Windows 8.1 Enterprise to Windows 10 Pro, the upgrade process will retain your personal files but will not upgrade your apps and settings.

6. Touch **Next**. Setup checks for updates again.

7. If setup detects any issues with the proposed upgrade, you are informed now. Acknowledge any unimportant messages by touching **OK**.

8. Setup now checks for available hard disk space and then prompts you to continue. Touch **Install** when ready. Setup proceeds through the upgrade. When complete, you are prompted to sign in.

---

[5] *If you do not have a Microsoft account, go here:* *https://signup.live.com/signup*

[6] *Microsoft have indicated that users of specific versions of Windows 7 and Windows 8 can obtain a free upgrade by using the Windows Store. You can read about how to perform this assisted upgrade here: http://www.microsoft.com/en-us/windows/windows-10-upgrade*

[7] *A clean installation wipes the computer of apps and data. This is probably NOT what you want.*

Chapter 2

Navigating the Interface

What you will do in this chapter:

- Use touch to navigate the user interface
- Use the mouse to navigate the user interface
- Use keyboard shortcuts to navigate the user interface

Navigating with Touch

Before looking any further at using Windows 10, we should probably cover some basics in navigation. I am assuming that you have Windows 10 installed on a touch device, so for the most part, my instructions throughout the book will be based on that assumption.

Note: If you do not have touch, then during procedures in this book, click instead of touching and right-click instead of touch and holding.

Signing in

When you see the initial Windows splash screen, swipe up with your finger from the bottom of the screen.

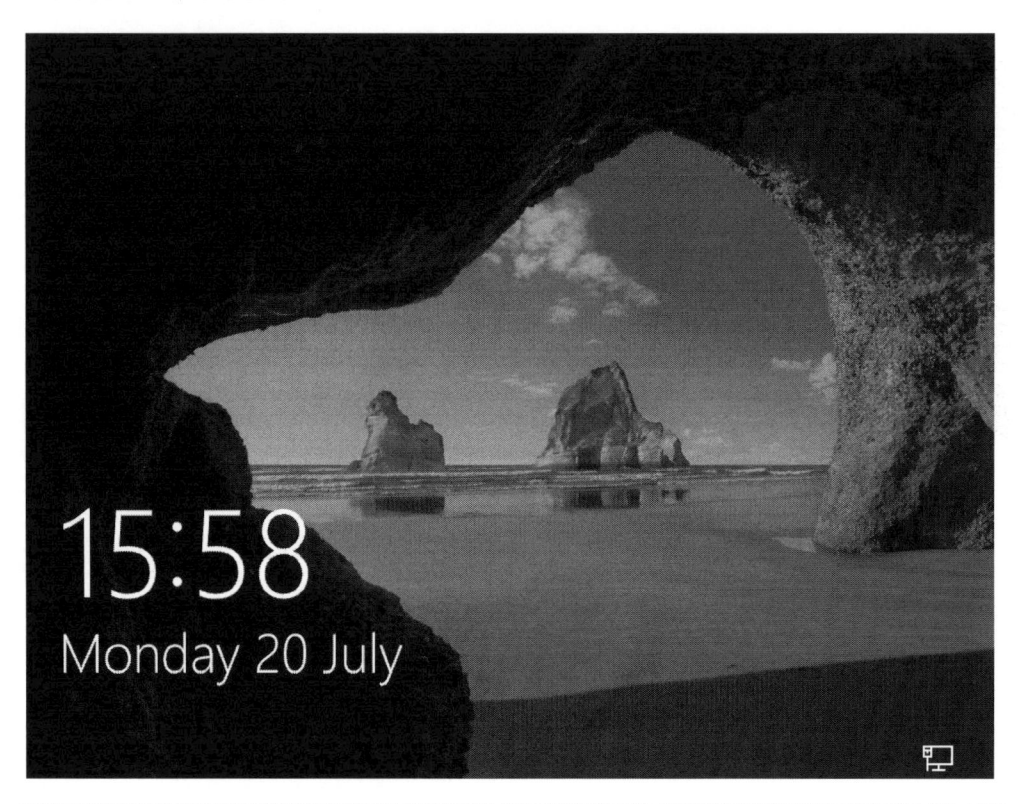

Figure 8.– Windows 10 splash screen

You should now see the sign in page. Touch your finger into the **Password** box and the virtual keyboard will appear. Now type your password. Then you can either hit Enter on the virtual keyboard, or else touch the arrow to the right of the

Chapter 2 - Navigating the Interface

Password box. Windows will sign you into your device. You may be prompted to enable PIN sign in the first time you sign in to Windows 10.

Note: You can enable or disable this feature at any time through Settings later.

If you enable PIN sign in, you must enter a PIN instead of your password during subsequent sign in attempts.

Note: Windows 10 supports something called Windows Hello. This new feature enables you to sign in by using facial recognition. However, your device must be equipped with an infrared camera enabling it to differentiate between a photo and the real you. If this is an important feature for you, make sure your device has the appropriate type of camera.

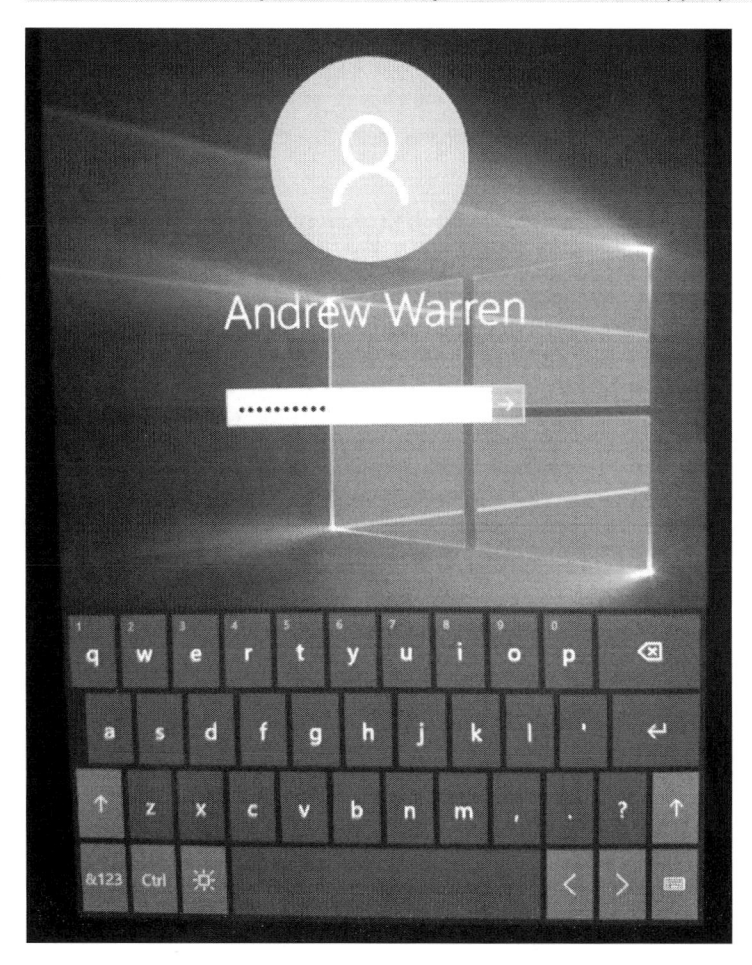

Figure 9.– Windows sign in screen

Note: You can sign in with a local account or with a Microsoft Account. For information on using a Microsoft Account, see the next chapter. You can also sign in with a domain account if your device is connected to your workplace network. We will not be discussing domain accounts, nor domains, in this book.

Chapter 2 - Navigating the Interface

Accessing Start

To access Start, touch the capacitive or physical Start button on your device. This will usually be below the display on the center point of the device bezel. Alternatively, touch **Start** on the lower left of the taskbar.

Figure 10.– Capacitive Start button

The appearance of Start will vary depending upon whether you are running Windows on a tablet or non-touch device. Shown below is the Start screen as it appears for a touch device, with the Start screen filling the whole display – i.e. maximized.

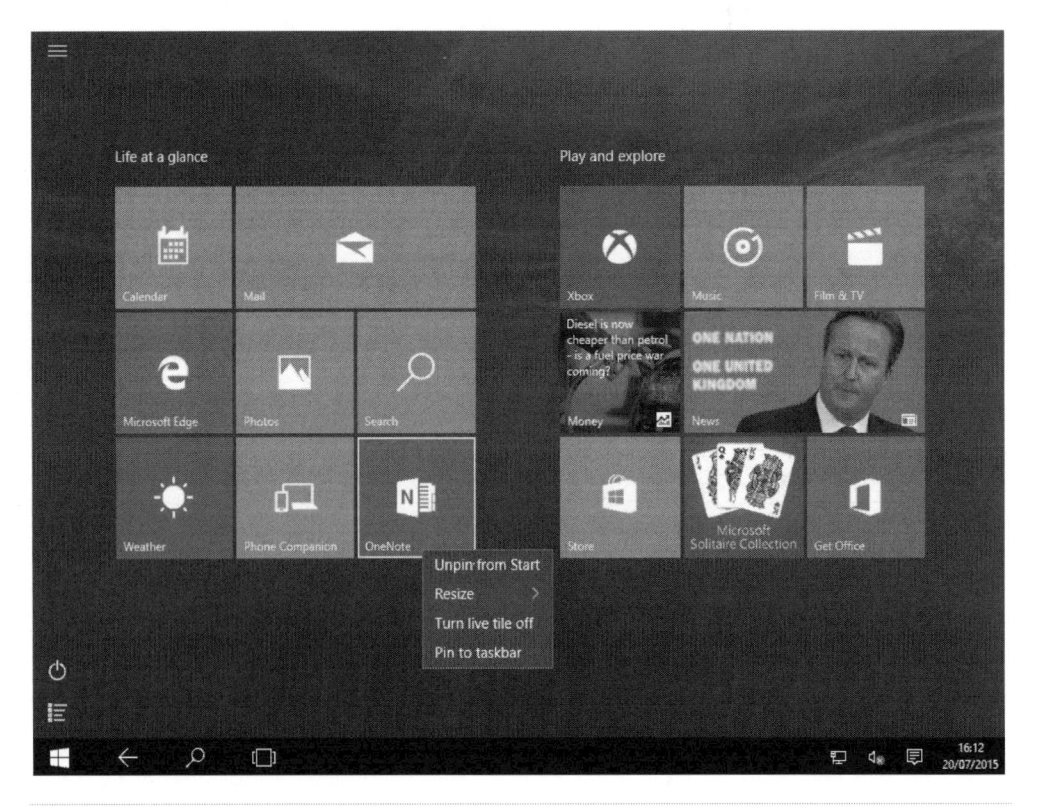

Figure 11.– Start screen on a tablet

Chapter 2 - Navigating the Interface

Customizing Start

Figure 12.– Navigation elements on Start

You have a great deal of control over the appearance of Start. You can add and remove tiles, change their location and size, and enable or disable live tile updates[8].

---

[8] *Live updates are tiles that display updating information, such as with weather and news app tiles.*

Chapter 2 - Navigating the Interface

Adding tiles

From **Start**, touch **All apps** in the lower left corner. Use your finger to glide up and down the list of apps on the left.

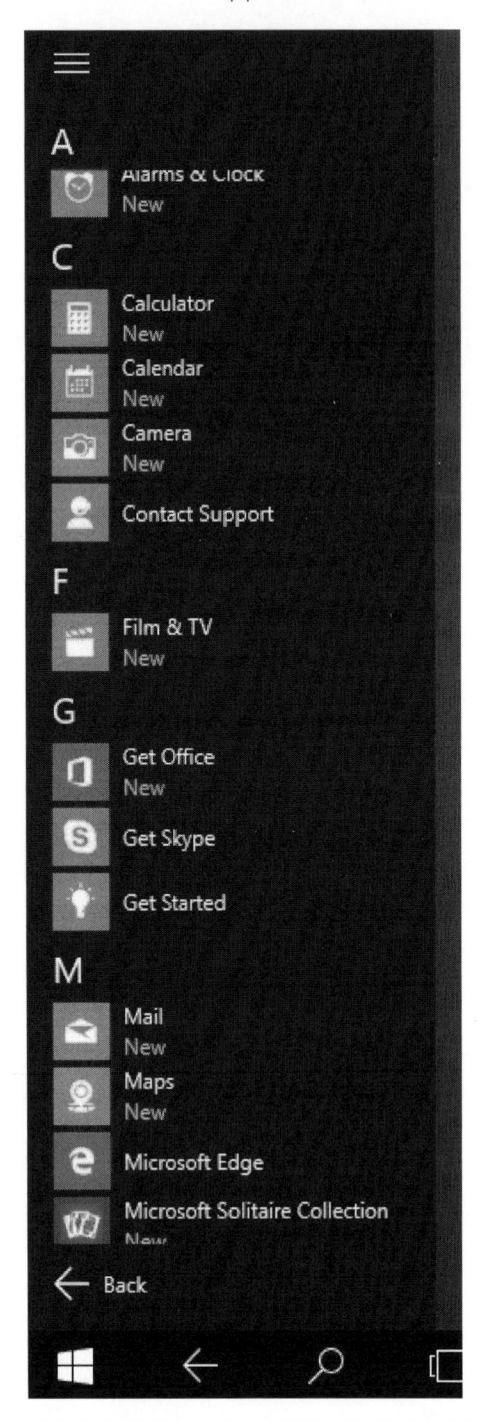

Figure 13.– All apps list

Chapter 2 - Navigating the Interface

When you locate the app you want, touch and hold the app, and then from the context menu, touch **Pin to Start** or **Pin to taskbar**, as appropriate.

Figure 14.– Pin to Start

Resizing tiles

To resize a tile, touch and hold the tile, and then touch the ellipse button (three dots in a white circle). From the context menu, touch the appropriate size.

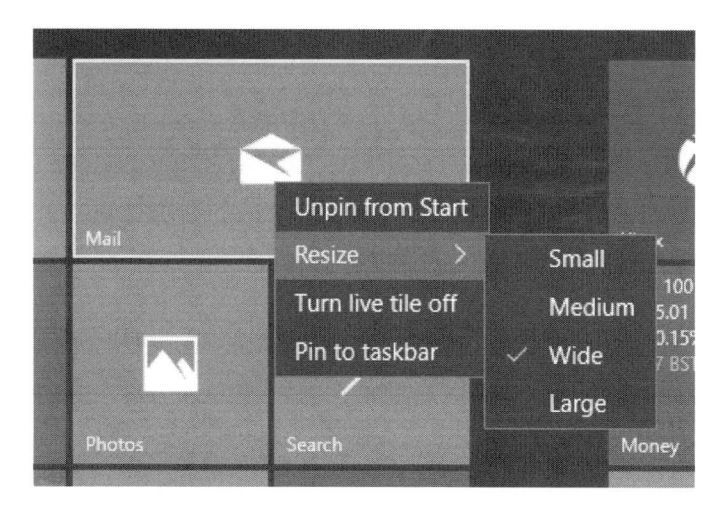

Figure 15.– Resize a tile

Removing tiles

To remove a tile from Start, locate the tile and touch and hold it. Click the pin symbol. The tile is removed. Note that this does not uninstall the app.

Grouping tiles

You will notice that the tiles are grouped automatically. You can move tiles between groups. Touch and hold a tile you want to move and then drag the tile to the new group. Release the tile.

You can move groups on the screen, too. Touch and hold the group name, and then drag the group to a new position on the Start screen and release it.

To rename a group, touch and hold the group name and when the virtual keyboard appears, type the new name and press Enter.

To create a new group, drag a tile to an unused area of the Start screen and release it. This creates an unnamed group. You can now rename the group using the instructions shown above.

Using the preceding actions, you can add, create, and customize groups on the Start screen so that your tiles are grouped in meaningful ways for you.

Figure 16.– Groups

Chapter 2 - Navigating the Interface

Accessing Settings

Windows 10 has consolidated many of the settings and configuration options and made them accessible from a single place, Settings. You can access settings by touching the **Settings** shortcut on the Start menu.

Figure 17.– Settings on the Start screen

Alternatively, swipe in from the right-hand side of your display to bring up **Action Centre**[9] and then touch **All settings**. We'll talk more about Action Centre later.

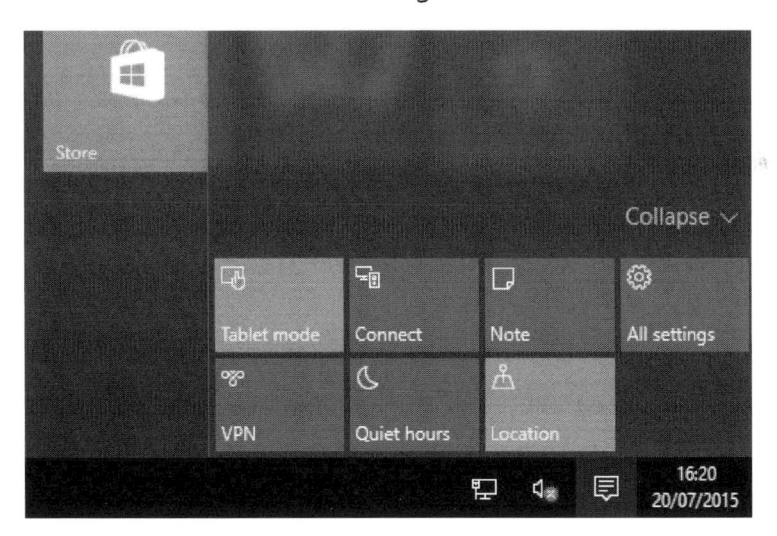

Figure 18.– Action Centre tiles

Almost all Windows settings are accessible through one of the categories shown[10]. For instance, if you want to configure display options, touch **System**. You can then configure the desired settings.

---

[9] Action Centre is the text bubble visible on the right of the taskbar.
[10] Some advanced settings are available from Control Panel. I'll call those out as we progress.

Chapter 2 - Navigating the Interface

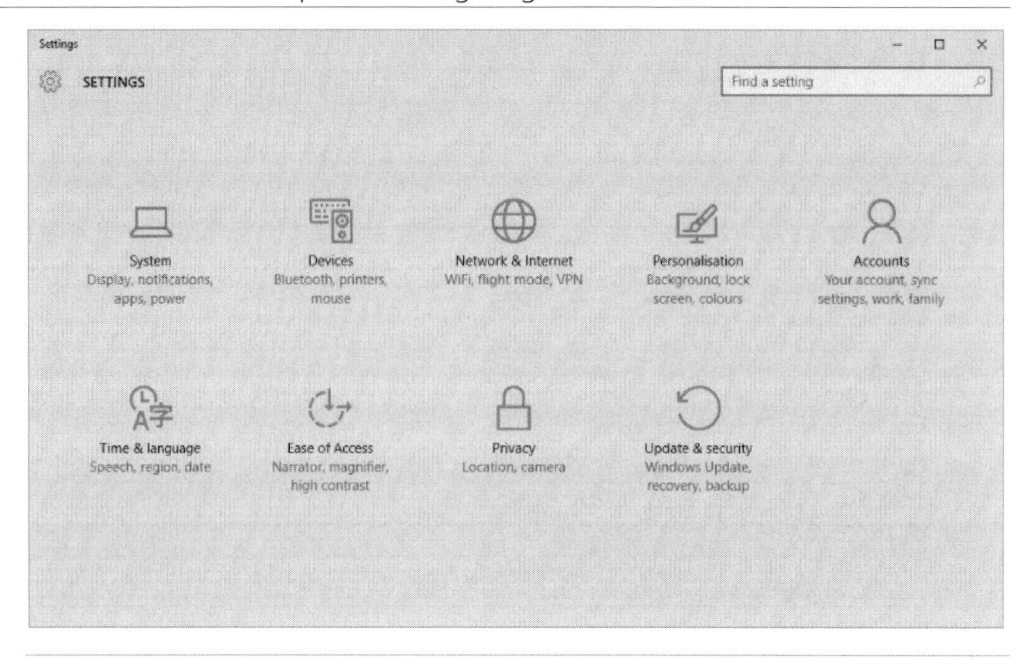

Figure 19.– Settings

Note: For those of you familiar with earlier versions of Windows, there is still a Control Panel in Windows 10. There is also a Computer Management tool. These should only be used by more experienced users. In any event, most configuration changes can be easily accomplished using Settings.

Chapter 2 - Navigating the Interface

Navigating With a Mouse and Keyboard

It is possible to use a mouse and a keyboard to navigate the interface, and for users of desktop computers, that may still be the best option. The procedure differs only slightly when navigating with a mouse and keyboard.

Signing in

After turning on your device, when you see the Windows splash screen, to display the sign in screen, you can either click anywhere on the screen with your mouse, or else you can press CTRL+ALT+DEL on your keyboard. Then type your password into the **Password** box and press Enter.

Accessing Start

To access Start, click the **Start** button on the lower left of the taskbar, or else press the Windows key (⊞)on your keyboard.

Customizing Start

You can perform the same customizations with a mouse as you can with touch.

- **Adding tiles**. To add a tile from the apps list, click **All apps** at the bottom of Start, and then scroll down the apps list. Right-click the appropriate app and then click **Pin to Start** or **Pin to taskbar** as required.

- **Resizing tiles**. In Start, right-click the appropriate tile and from the context menu, point to **Resize**, and then click the size you want.

- **Removing tiles**. In Start, right-click the appropriate tile and from the context menu, click Unpin from Start. This does not uninstall the app.

- **Grouping tiles**. You can create groups by dragging a tile to an unused area of Start. To rename this or any other group, click in the title bar of the group and then type the name.

Accessing Settings

To access Settings, from **Start**, click **Settings** in the **Apps** list. Then click the appropriate tile for the setting you want.

If you are on the desktop, click **Notifications** in the taskbar and then click **All settings**.

Chapter 2 - Navigating the Interface

Using Shortcut Keys

Although using touch, when available, and/or a mouse is probably the easiest way to navigate the Windows 10 operating system, as with earlier versions of Windows, you can also use just the keyboard to navigate. For instance, by pressing the Windows key (⊞) on your keyboard, you will switch to the Start screen, or back to the desktop, depending upon your start point.

Here are some of the more common keyboard shortcuts.

- **Windows + I.** Opens Settings.
- **Windows + R.** Opens the Run window, enabling you to type the name of an app that you want to launch.
- **Windows + E.** File Explorer opens.
- **Windows + D.** Show the desktop.
- **Windows + E.** File Explorer opens.
- **Windows + L.** Lock your computer.

There are many other keyboard shortcuts, and as we progress through the book, where relevant, I shall call them out.

Note: Using shortcut keys, or navigating with a physical keyboard, assumes that you have a keyboard. We'll discuss how to attach peripherals, such as Bluetooth keyboards, later in this book.

Chapter 3

Connecting to the Internet

What you will do in this chapter:

- Connect to networks
- Create and use a Microsoft Account
- Learn about OneDrive
- Configure sync settings

Managing Network Connections

Before you can do pretty much anything, you must connect your device to the Internet. In reality, that just means connecting it to your wireless hub at home.

Note: The specific details for connecting to home hubs varies depending on the vendor of the hub, and who your telecom provider is. The steps I have used for guidance are based on using a BT Home Hub, but most other hubs will be pretty similar.

Things you need before you start

- **Wireless SSID**. Start by obtaining the Wireless SSID. This is the advertised name of the hub; that is, the name the hub uses to announce itself. You will find this printed on the hub somewhere. BT also provide a small plastic card that has this information.

- **Wireless key**. This network security key is the 'password' that you will need to connect to the hub. Again, it will be printed on the hub somewhere.

Establishing a wireless connection

Once you have the required information, use the following procedure to connect to your network.

1. Open **Settings**. From the desktop, swipe in from the right, and then touch **All settings**. Alternatively, from Start, touch **Settings** in the **Apps** list.

Chapter 3 - Connecting to the Internet

2. In Settings, touch **Network & Internet**.

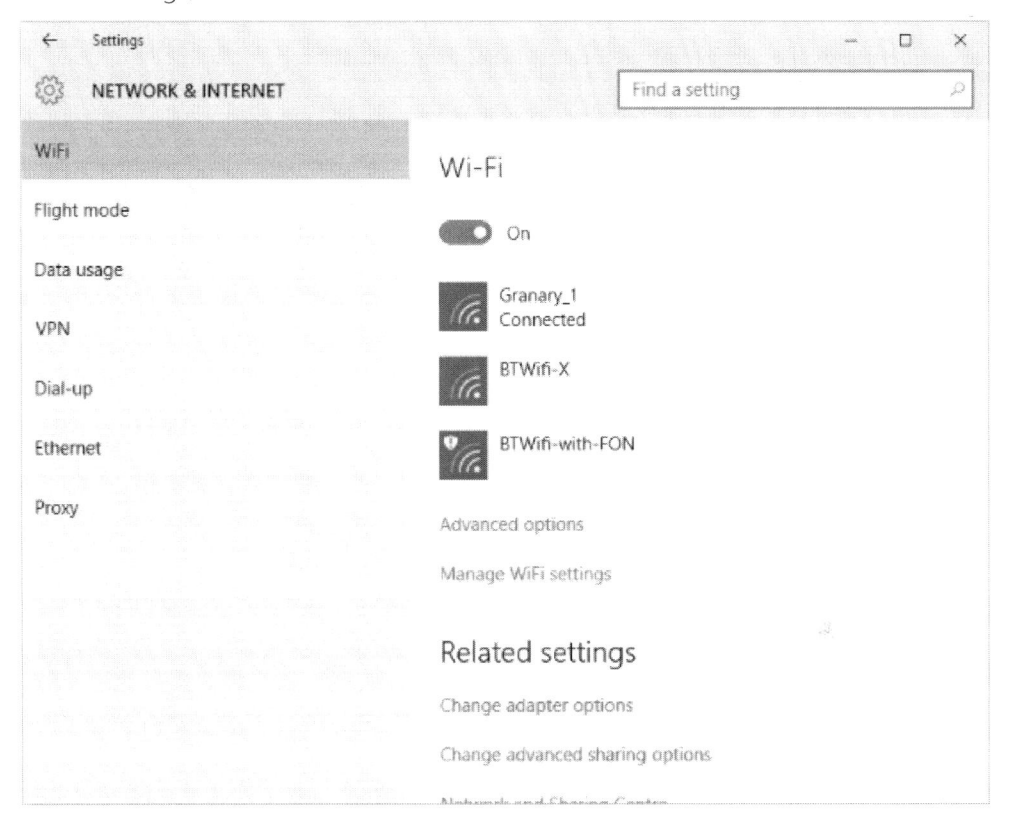

Figure 20.– Wi-Fi options

3. You should be able to see a list of Wi-Fi networks. The list may contain only one Wi-Fi network or in may contain several, depending on what your device can see. Touch the network that has the SSID you recorded earlier.

Chapter 3 - Connecting to the Internet

4. Select **Connect automatically** and then touch **Connect**.

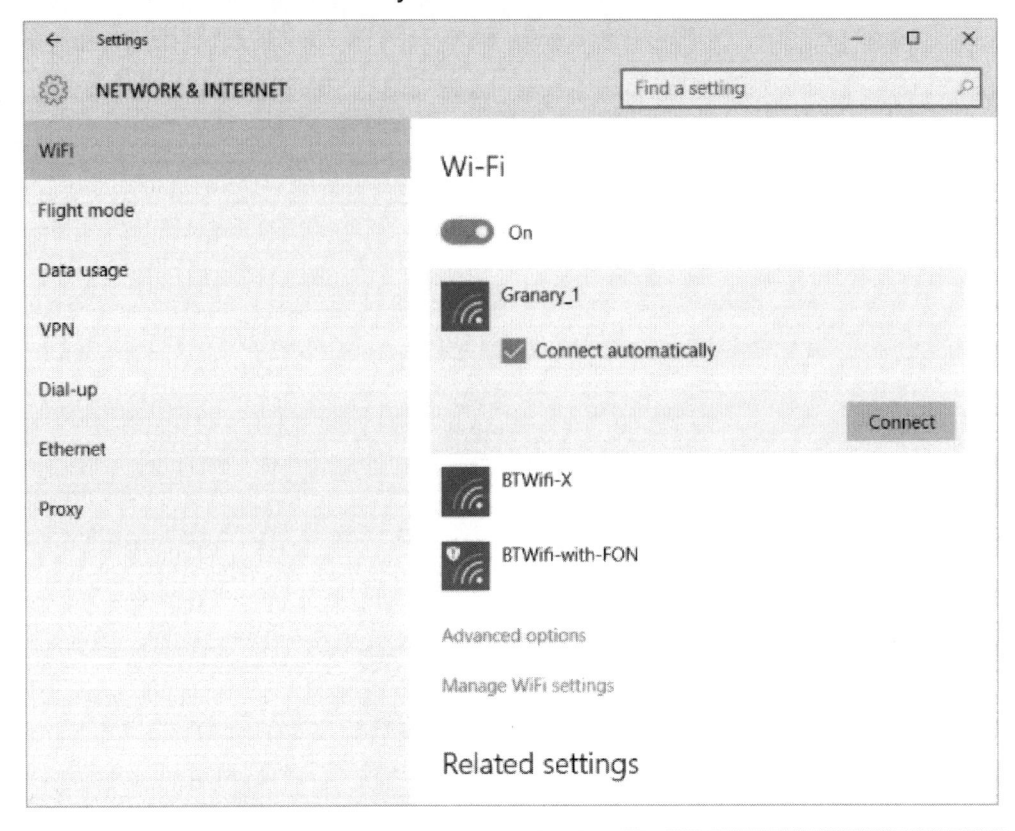

Figure 21.– Connecting to a Wi-Fi network

Chapter 3 - Connecting to the Internet

5. You are prompted for the security key. Enter the key you recorded earlier into the text box and then touch **Next**. Assuming the key you entered is correct, you should now be connected to your wireless hub and, in turn, to the Internet.

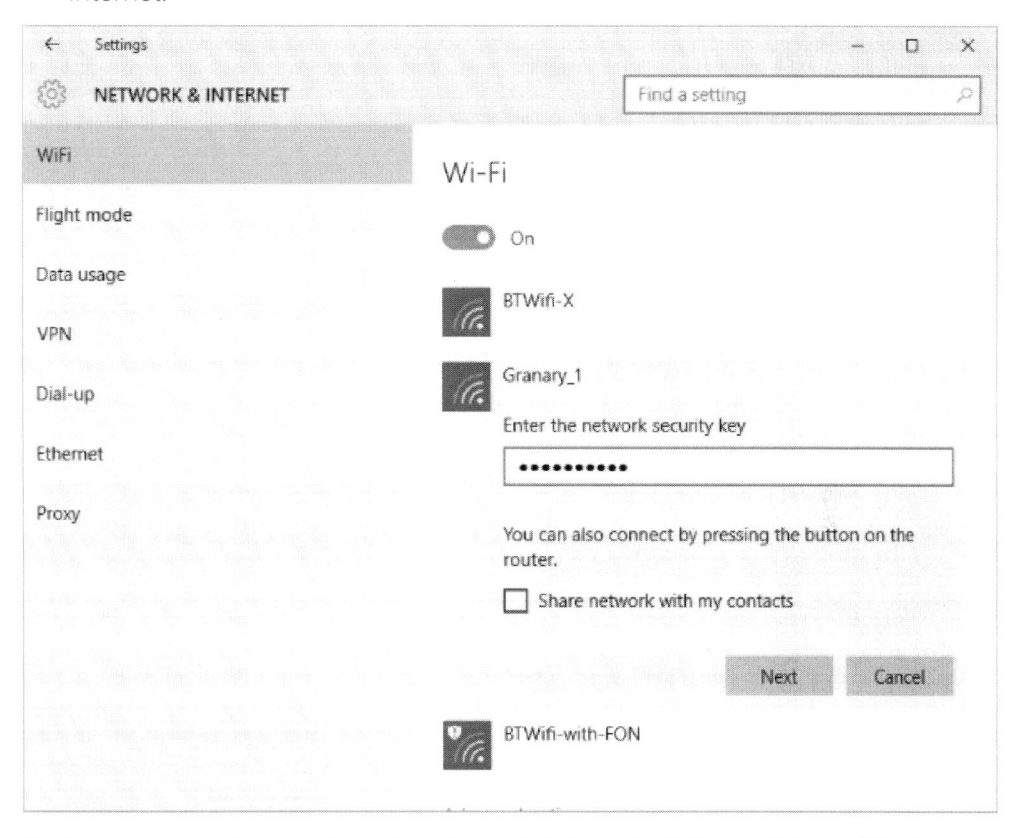

Figure 22.– Entering a security key

Note: Some hubs (although not the BT Home hubs) require that when you connect a new device, you must also press a physical button on the hub to acknowledge the connection attempt. This is an additional security precaution.

Chapter 3 - Connecting to the Internet

Managing your wireless connection

When you have established your network connection, you can view or configure its properties by touching the wireless icon in the system tray on the taskbar[11]. You can then touch:

- **Disconnect**. You can disconnect from any wireless network.

- **Connect**. A list of SSIDs are displayed here. You can choose to connect to an alternate network using the procedure above.

- **Network settings**. View all network settings. This enables you to access the **Network & Internet** shortcut from **Settings**.

- **Wi-Fi**. Click this button to disable/enable the Wi-Fi radio in your device.

- **Flight mode**. Click this button to enable/disable all radios in your device making it safe for flight.

Figure 23.– Managing Wi-Fi connections

---

[11] *The system tray is on the extreme right of the taskbar.*

Chapter 3 - Connecting to the Internet

Using a Microsoft Account

What is a Microsoft account?

When you use a Windows 10 device, you can sign in using a local account. This identifies you as a user to the local device only. It does not allow you to identify yourself to others on the Internet, or to services on the Internet, such as Microsoft Office 365™, OneDrive, Skype®, or email, such as Outlook.com, and others.

Note: During setup of your device, you may be prompted to create and connect a Microsoft account to your device. This assumes your device is connected to the Internet during the setup process. If you are prompted to do this, I recommend that you do so.

When you use a Microsoft account, it enables you to identify yourself to Internet-based services, to purchase and download apps from the Windows Store, and to sync your settings between devices.

Creating a Microsoft account

Use the following procedure to create a Microsoft account.

1. Switch to **Settings**.
2. Touch **Accounts**.

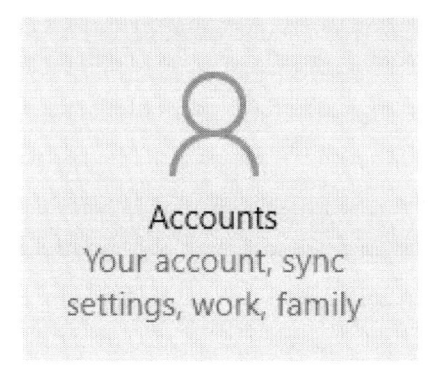

Accounts
Your account, sync settings, work, family

Figure 24.– Accounts

Chapter 3 - Connecting to the Internet

3. Touch **Sign in with a Microsoft account instead**.

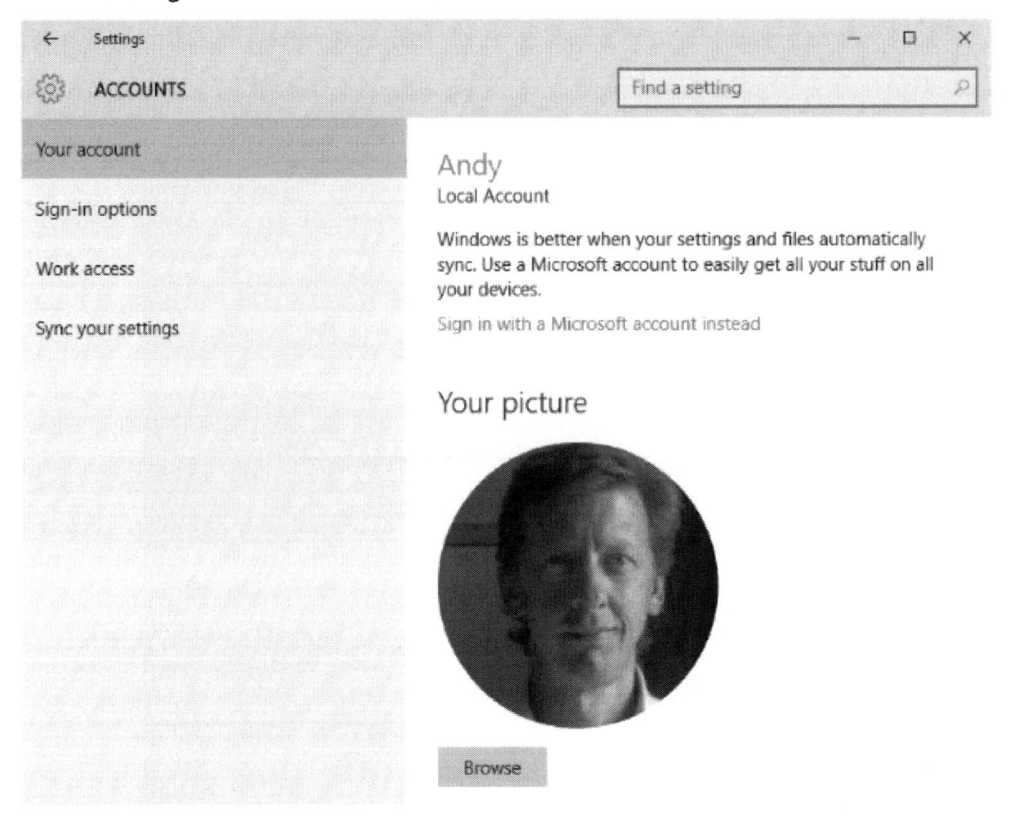

Figure 25.– Your account

4. Enter the password for the local account and touch **Next**.

Chapter 3 - Connecting to the Internet

5. If you already have a Microsoft account, enter the credentials now. Otherwise, if you do not have a Microsoft account, touch **Create one**.

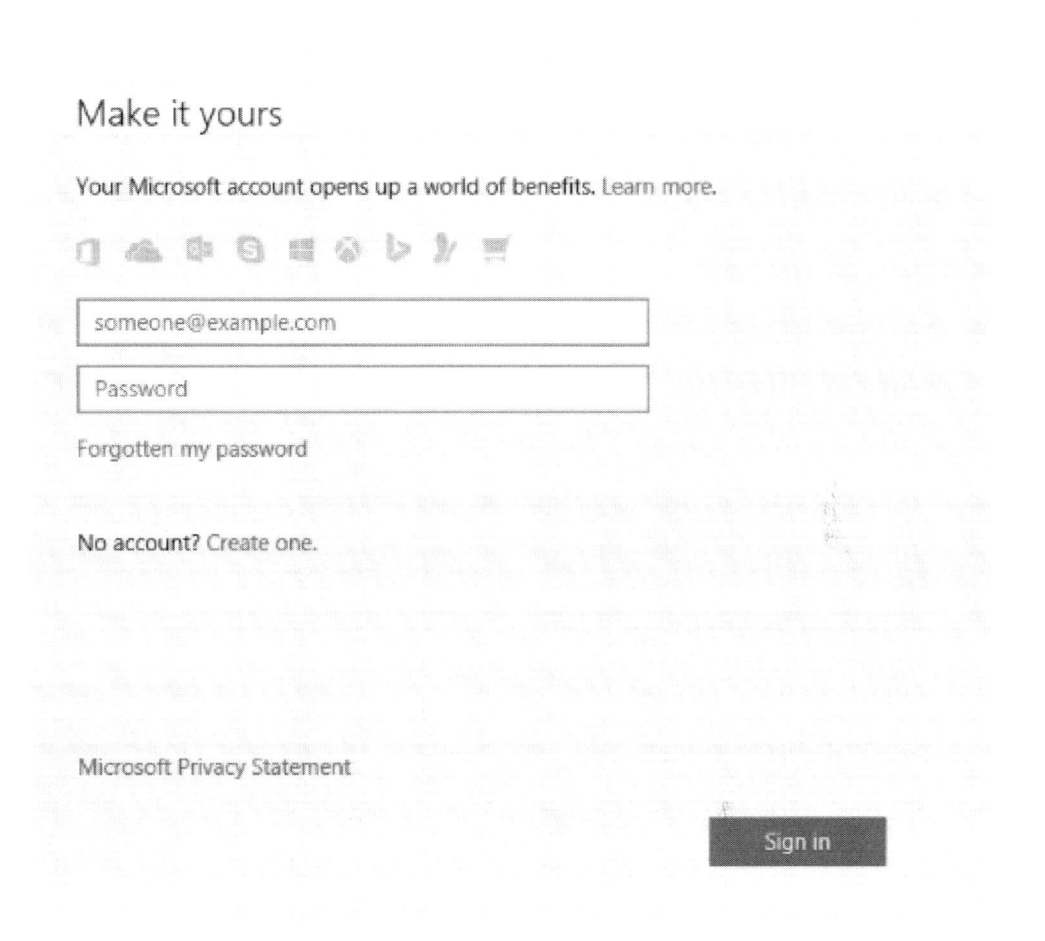

Figure 26.– Sign in to your Microsoft account

Chapter 3 - Connecting to the Internet

6. Enter your **First name** and **Surname**.

7. If you do not have an email address, touch **Get a new email address**. If you have an existing email address that you want to use, enter that email address.

8. Enter a password. This password is used to sign you into your account, so don't forget it. Touch **Next**.

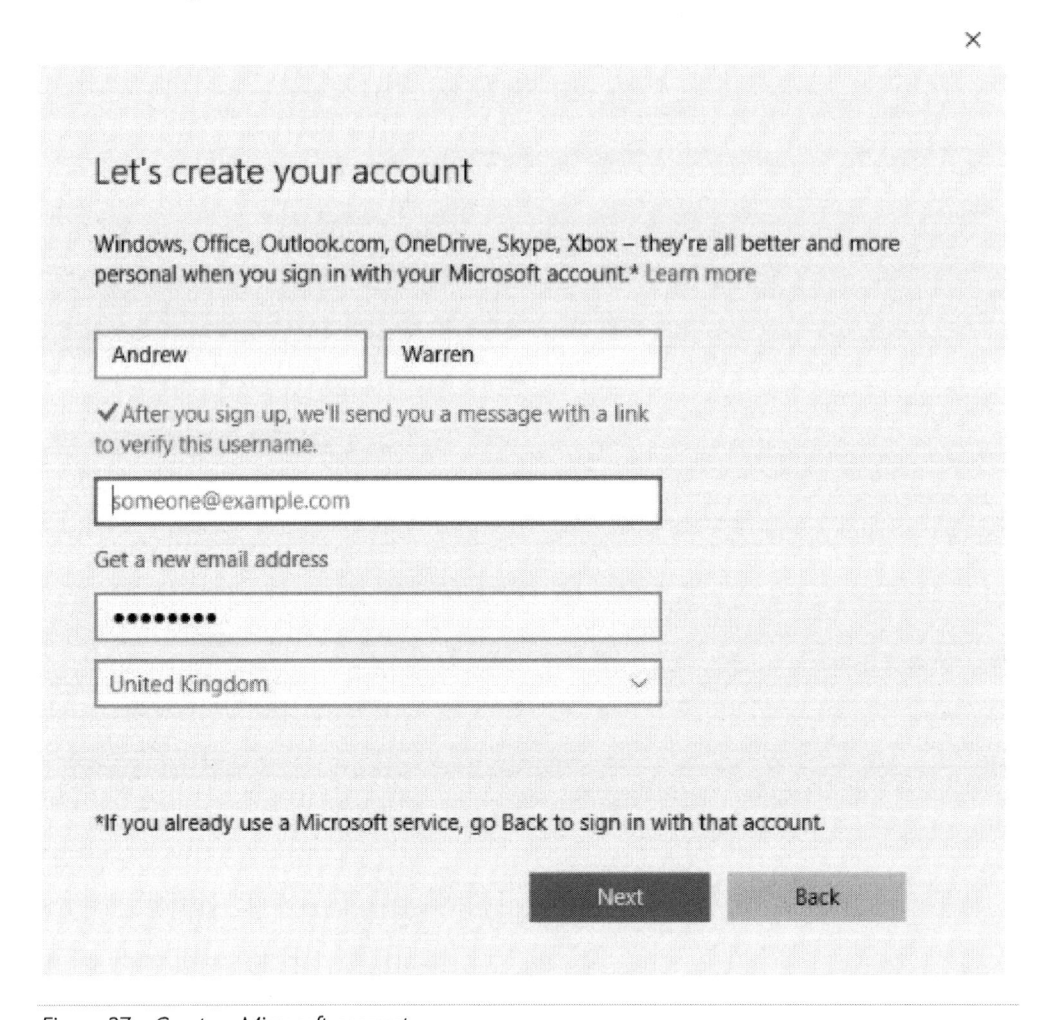

Figure 27.– Create a Microsoft account

Chapter 3 - Connecting to the Internet

9. Your Microsoft account is created and an email is sent to the email address you specified. This is used for two-factor authentication[12]. You will need access to this email message. You are returned to the **Your account** page. Touch **Verify**.

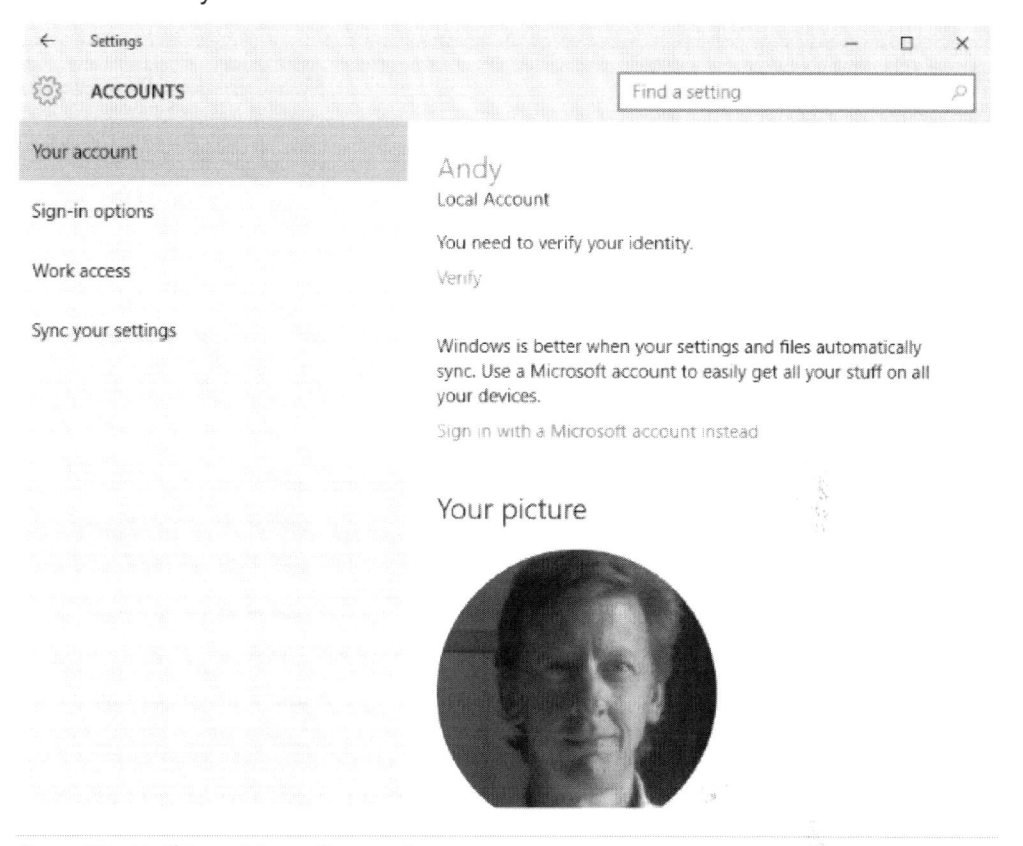

Figure 28.– Verifying a Microsoft account

---

[12] *Two-factor authentication works by using two of three factors about you to verify your identity. Something you know (such as a password), something you have (such as a phone number or an email address), and something you are (such a biometric factors – fingerprints, retina scans and so on).*

Chapter 3 - Connecting to the Internet

10. Open the email you were sent. It contains links that you can click to verify your account. Alternatively, make a note of the security code in the message, and then on the **Verify email** page, enter the code and touch **Next**.

Figure 29.– Enter verification code

11. Sign out, and then sign in using your Microsoft account. Use the email address you specified as the User name and the password you specified as the password.

That's it. You've created and verified your Microsoft account and linked it to your Windows 10 device.

Using OneDrive

What is OneDrive?

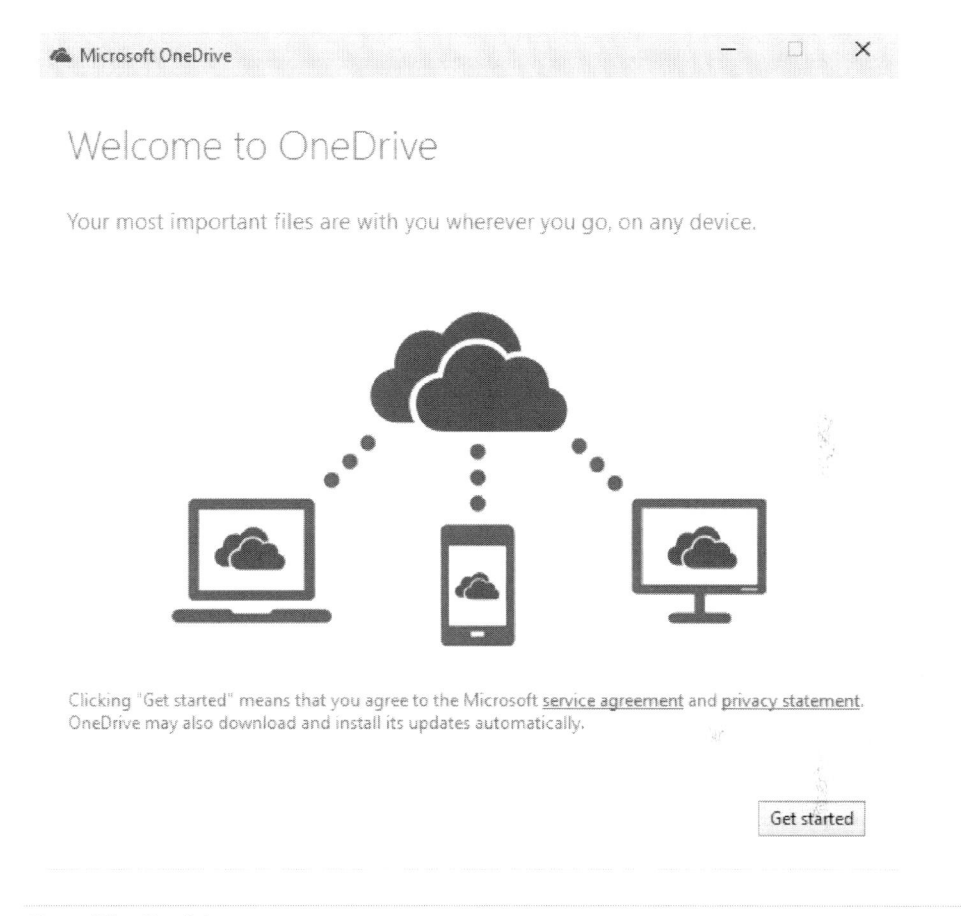

Figure 30.– OneDrive

OneDrive is a free storage area provided to all users of Microsoft accounts. Often, users of Outlook.com, or of Office 365 receive OneDrive space. You can use this space to securely store your files – any of your files – to save using local storage. This has the added benefit of the content being available between your various devices. For example, if you store your music files in OneDrive, you can access your music library from your Windows Phone, your tablet, and your laptop.

OneDrive is embedded into Windows 10. When you attempt to save a document using an app, such as Microsoft Office Word, you can select OneDrive as a location. You can also see OneDrive in File Explorer.

Chapter 3 - Connecting to the Internet

The first time you sign in to Windows 10 with your Microsoft account, or subsequently attempt to access OneDrive storage from Windows (for example, clicking OneDrive in File Explorer), you are prompted to run a setup program. This simple, wizard-driven program guides you through the process of setting up your OneDrive space.

1. When prompted, enter your **Microsoft account name** and **Password** and touch **Sign in**.
2. When the Welcome to OneDrive wizard starts, touch **Get started**.
3. At the **Introducing your OneDrive folder** page, touch **Next**.

Figure 31.– Introducing your OneDrive folder

Note: You can change the local cache location of your OneDrive content, but this is not usually necessary.

Chapter 3 - Connecting to the Internet

4. At the **Sync your OneDrive files to this PC** page, touch **Next**.

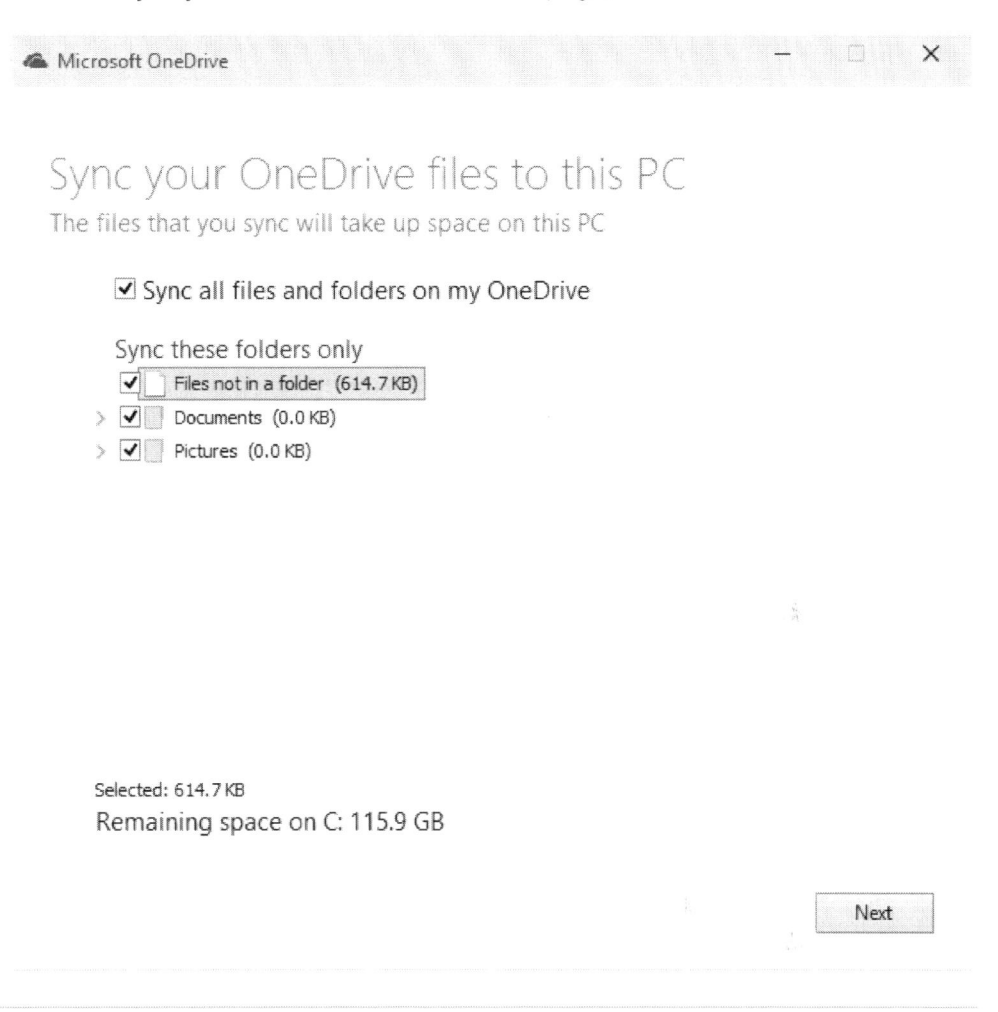

Figure 32.– Sync your OneDrive files to this PC

Note: You can choose to be selective over which type of files are synchronized. Unless you are sure about what you're doing, leave the default values as they are.

5. Finally, touch **Done**.

Chapter 3 - Connecting to the Internet

6. You may see a prompt from **User Account Control**. This security check is just making sure you are happy to make this significant system change. Touch **Yes**.

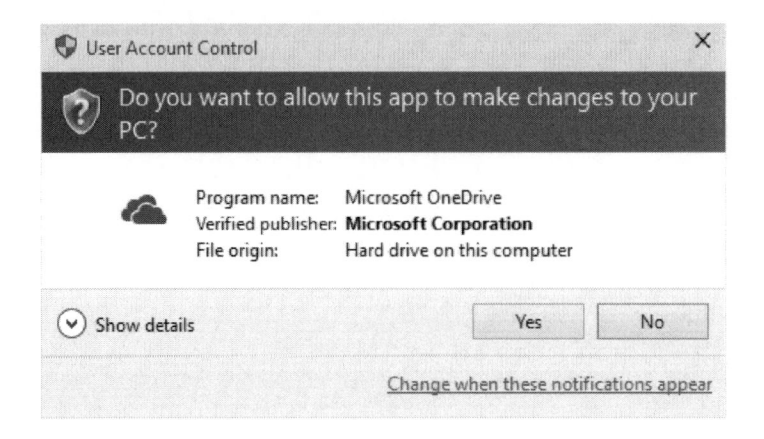

Figure 33.– User Account Control prompt

7. File Explorer opens and displays your OneDrive content.

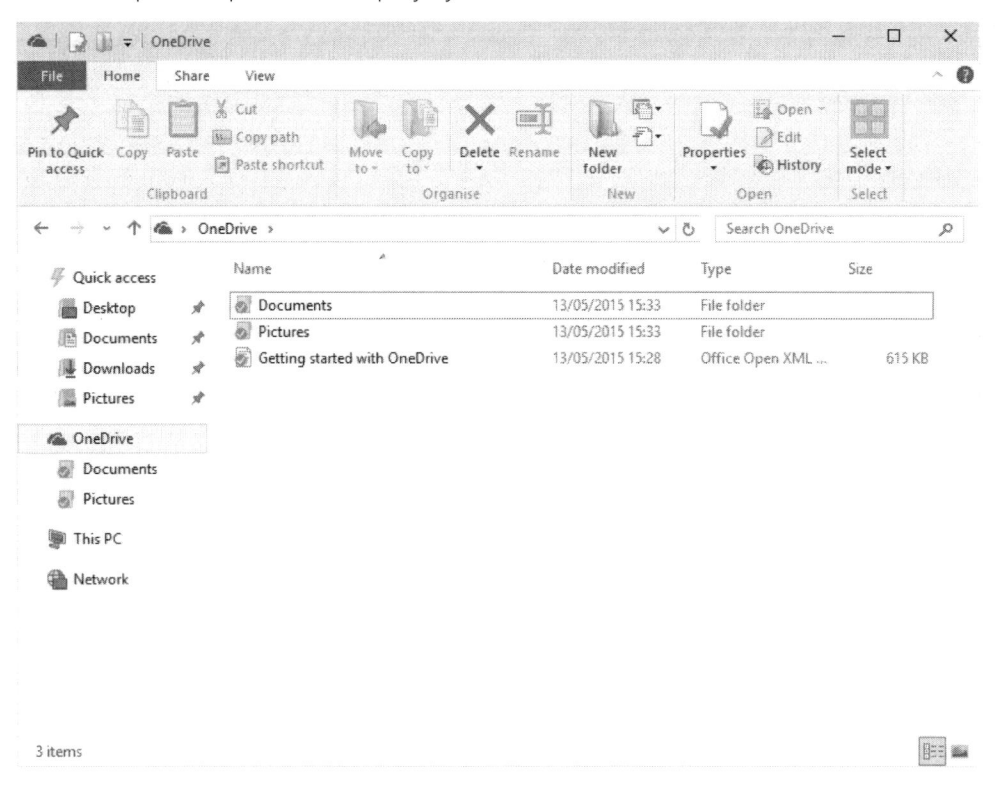

Figure 34.– OneDrive in File Explorer

Page - 48

Synchronizing Settings

One of the best things about using OneDrive is that you can sync your settings between Windows devices. Settings include:

- **Theme**. Stores the appearance settings of your device.
- **Web browser settings**. Is your Internet Explorer/Edge browser preferences, including things like favourites, and security settings.
- **Passwords**. Is the list of passwords you have used and chosen to store when accessing network locations and Internet sites. You are always prompted for Windows to store these passwords when you access a site[13].
- **Language preferences**. Keyboard and language preferences.
- **Ease of Access**. Accessibility settings, such as high contrast display and narrator.
- **Other Windows settings**. Miscellaneous Windows settings.

Once you have signed in with your Microsoft account and verified the account, Sync your settings is enabled by default. To change this, or reconfigure which settings are synced, open **Settings**, touch **Account**, and then touch **Sync your settings**.

---

[13] *You can review your stored passwords via the Credential Cache in Control Panel.*

Chapter 3 - Connecting to the Internet

Enable or disable the various settings as desired by using the On/Off buttons. If you don't want to sync any settings, touch **Sync settings** at the top of the list.

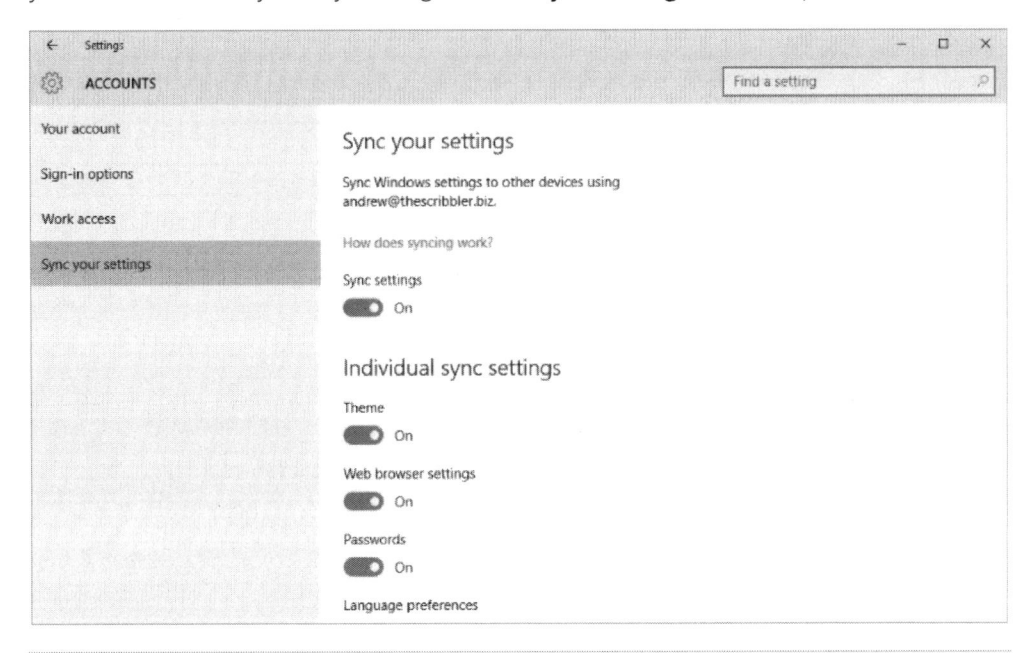

Figure 35.– Sync settings

When you use your Microsoft account to sign in at other devices, your settings will sync across.

Note: When you enable Sync your settings, the settings are stored in OneDrive in the OneDrive device backups area. You do not normally need to access this content directly via OneDrive.

Chapter 4

Customizing Windows

What you will do in this chapter:

- Personalise your device
- Configure display settings
- Configure tablet mode
- Use Notifications

Chapter 4 - Customizing Windows

Personalizing Your Device

Most users want to customize the way their device looks. This customization may include configuring a theme. A theme enables you to configure the way your device looks, including the background[14], colour scheme, and layout and options for the lock screen[15].

Choosing a theme

To configure a theme, or the individual elements of a theme, open **Settings**, and then touch **Personalization**. You can then choose to select a theme, or to separately configure the background, colours, Lock screen, and Start options.

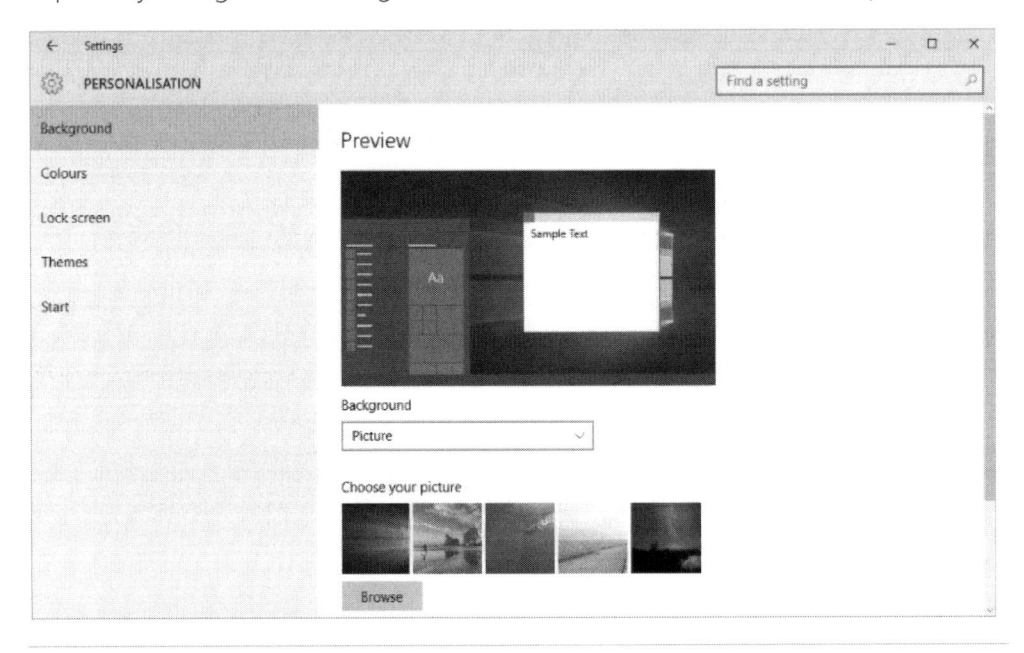

Figure 36.– Personalization options

---

[14] *Also known as wallpaper.*
[15] *The Lock screen is what is displayed on your device when it has locked after a period of inactivity.*

Chapter 4 - Customizing Windows

To select a theme:

1. Touch **Themes**. Touch **Theme settings**. Personalization options open in a new window.

2. Select from the available themes, or touch **Get more themes online**.

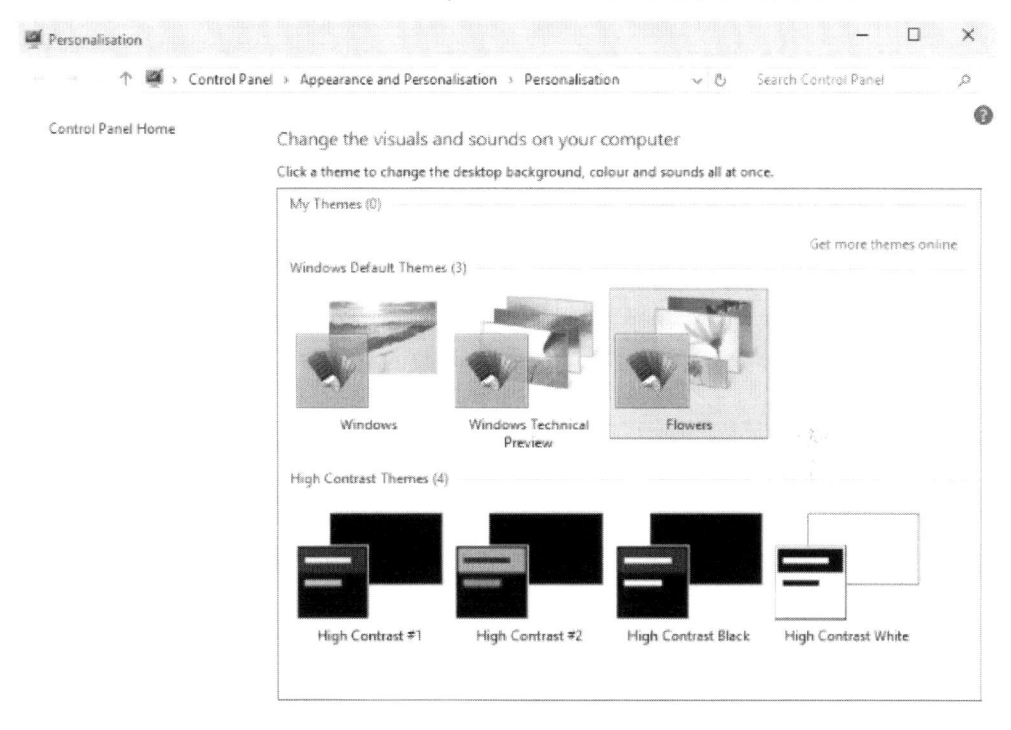

Figure 37.– Choosing a theme

3. When you are happy, close this window. You are now looking at the Personalization options again.

Chapter 4 - Customizing Windows

Choosing a colour scheme

To configure colours:

1. Touch **Colours**.
2. Turn off **Automatically pick an accent colour from my background**.
3. Click a suitable colour from the list.
4. Optionally, turn on **Show colour on Start, taskbar and action centre**.
5. Optionally, turn on **Make Start, taskbar and action centre transparent**.
6. If necessary, touch **High contrast settings**[16].

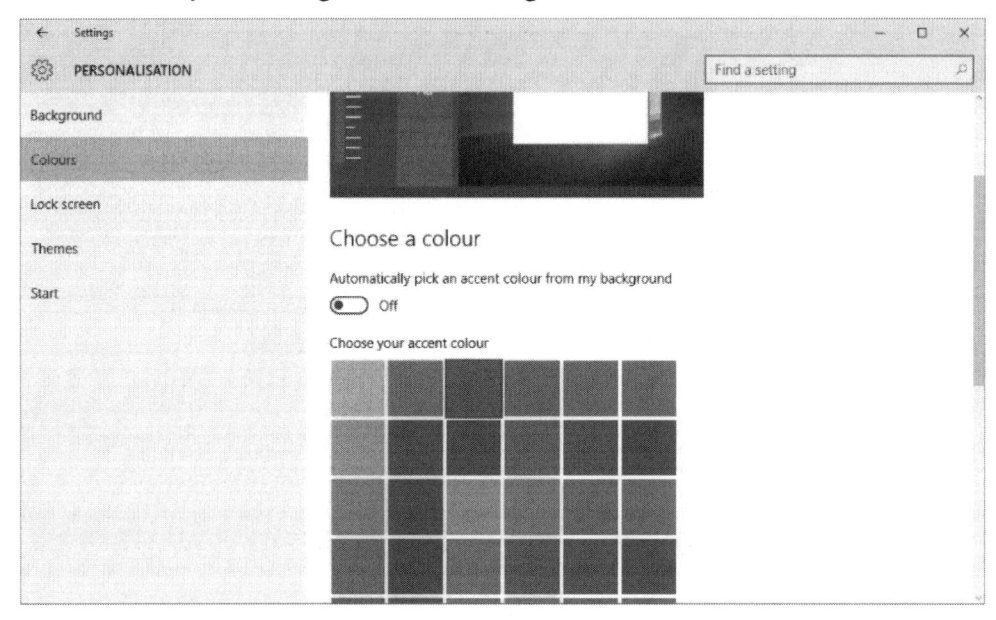

Figure 38.– Configuring colour options

---

[16] High contrast settings help users with visual impairments more easily navigate the user interface.

Chapter 4 - Customizing Windows

Configuring Lock screen options

To configure the lock screen:

1. Touch **Lock screen**.

2. In the **Background** list, touch **Picture** and then touch a suitable background. If you want to use a different picture from those displayed, touch **Browse** and locate your preferred picture. Once you have located your preferred picture in File Explorer, touch **Choose picture**. You are returned to Lock screen options.

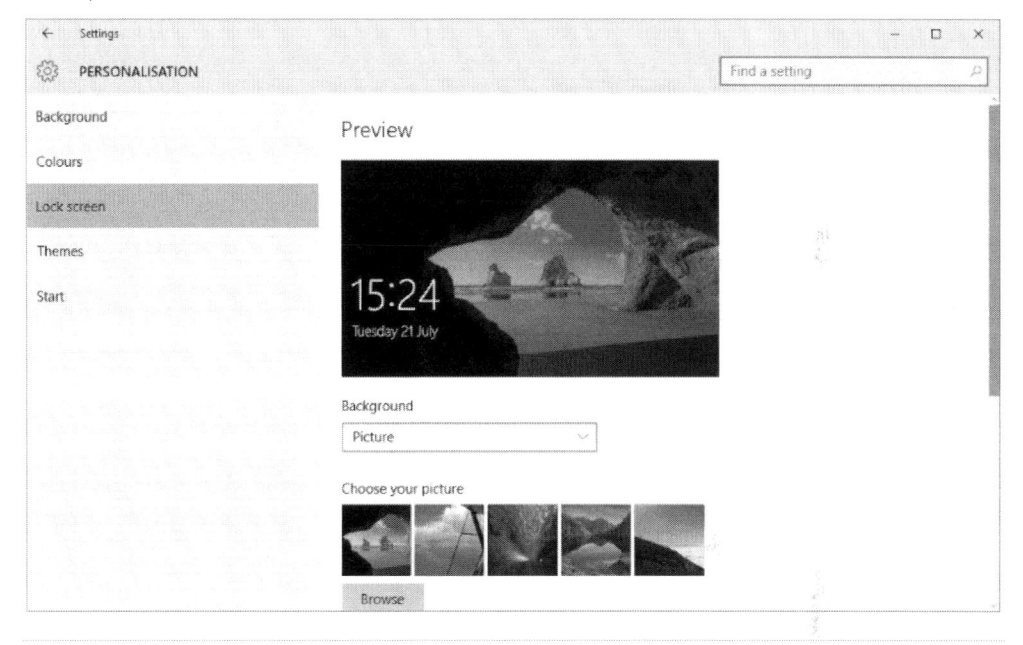

Figure 39.– Lock screen background

3. Beneath **Choose an app to display detailed status**, touch the icon shown.

Chapter 4 - Customizing Windows

4. In the **Choose an app** window, touch the app that you want to use. This app will display information in the lock screen.

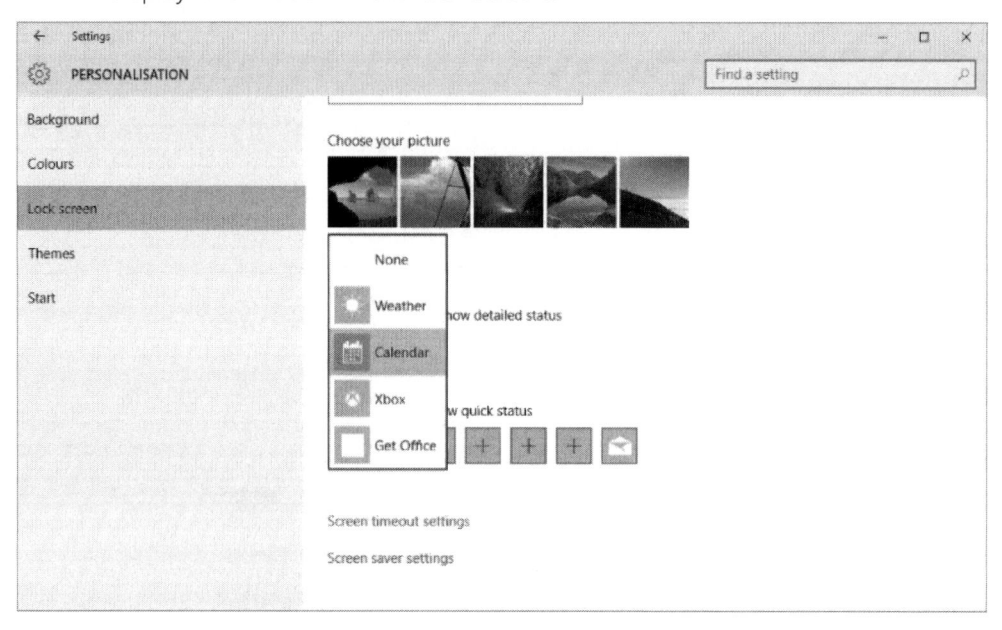

Figure 40.– Choosing an app to display detailed status on the lock screen

5. Optionally, touch the icons beneath **Choose apps to show quick status**. Then select the apps you want to use. These apps will display less detailed information on the lock screen.

Chapter 4 - Customizing Windows

6. Touch **Screen timeout settings**. You can now configure the way your device behaves during inactivity. Touch the drop down list for each behaviour and configure how long your device waits before turning off the screen or going to sleep[17].

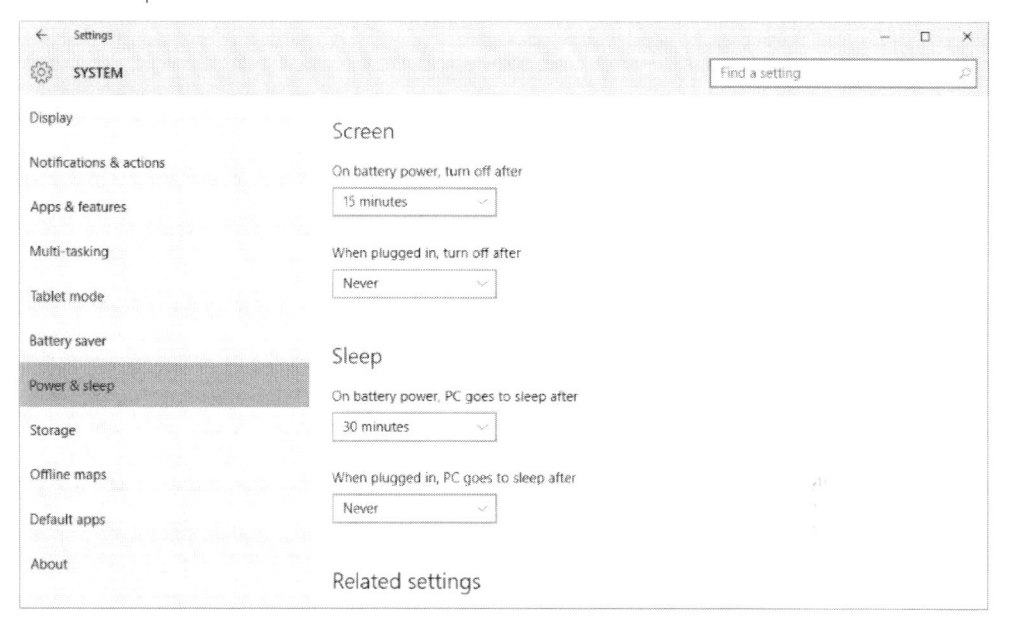

Figure 41.– Power & sleep options

7. When you have configured these options, touch the back button (the left pointing arrow next to System in the menu bar). You are in the main Settings window. Touch **Personalization** and touch **Lock screen**.

8. Touch **Screen saver settings** if you want a screensaver. Generally, this setting is irrelevant as it is better to put your device to sleep during inactivity.

Note: Remember that these settings will be synced between your devices.

---

[17] *Sleep keeps your device in its current state, but uses minimal power to maintain this state.*

Chapter 4 - Customizing Windows

Configuring Start options

To configure the options in Start:

1. Touch **Start**.

2. You can now configure the behaviour of the Start menu. This includes determining whether Start displays:

   - Most used apps
   - Recently added apps
   - Options about which folders appear in Start

3. Folders that you can display in Start are:

   - File Explorer (enabled by default)
   - Settings (enabled by default)
   - Documents
   - Downloads
   - Music
   - Pictures
   - Videos
   - HomeGroup

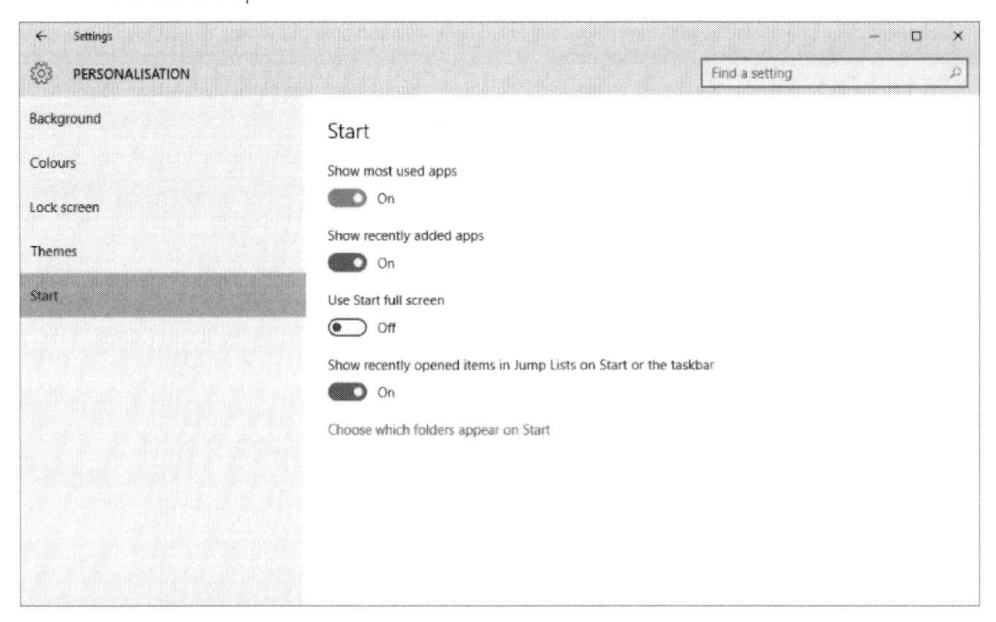

Figure 42.– Start options

Page - 58

Configuring Display Settings

The display settings control how your device uses the attached monitors. Clearly, if your device is a tablet, it will probably only have one monitor[18]. However, laptops and desktop devices support the attachment of additional monitors.

To configure display settings, open **Settings** and then touch **System**. Usually, you won't need to configure these settings unless you have attached an additional monitor, as shown below.

Figure 43.– Additional monitor detected by Windows

By default, the monitors are extended; that is, different information is displayed on each. You can, however, change this.

---

[18] *Some tablets enable you to attach secondary monitors via their Micro USB ports or Micro HDMI ports.*

Chapter 4 - Customizing Windows

1. In the **Multiple displays** list at the bottom of the screen, choose between **Duplicate these displays, Extend these displays, Show only on 1, Show Only on 2**. Touch **Apply**. Generally, you will choose **Extend these displays** as this enables you to display different content on each monitor.

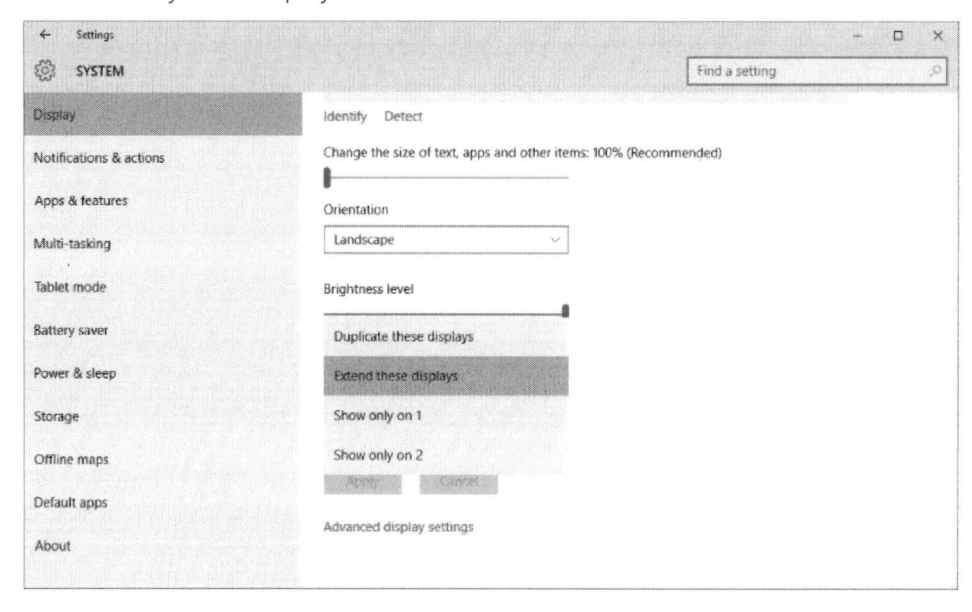

Figure 44.– Extending the displays

2. Scroll back up to the top of the window, and you can see the additional monitor. You can drag and drop the secondary monitor to reflect its physical location in relation to your primary monitor. This makes it much easier to use the monitor.

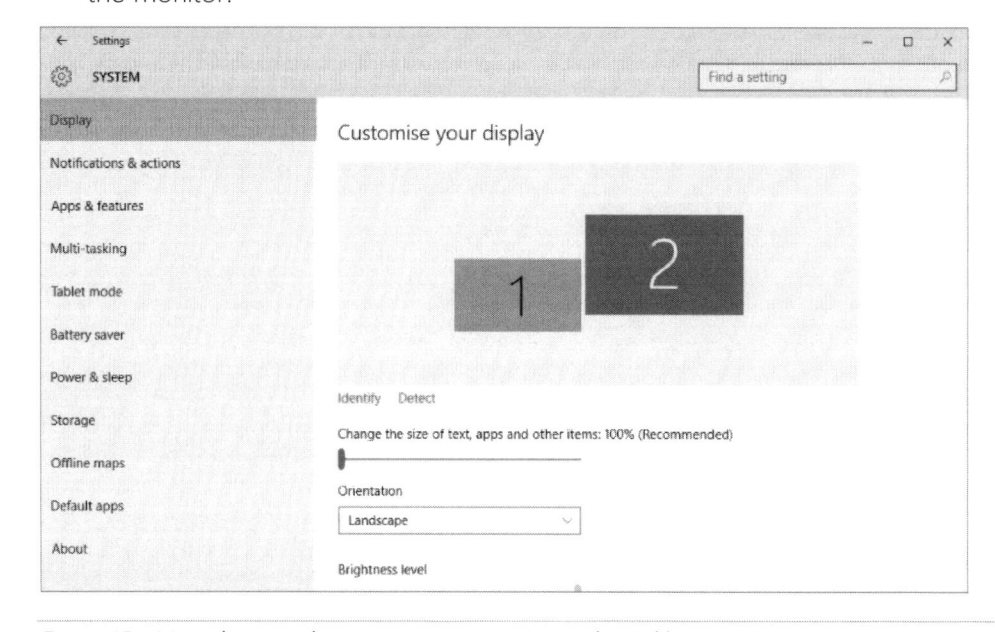

Figure 45.– Move the secondary monitor to represent its physical location

Chapter 4 - Customizing Windows

If you must exert more control over display options, at the bottom of the windows, touch **Advanced display settings**.

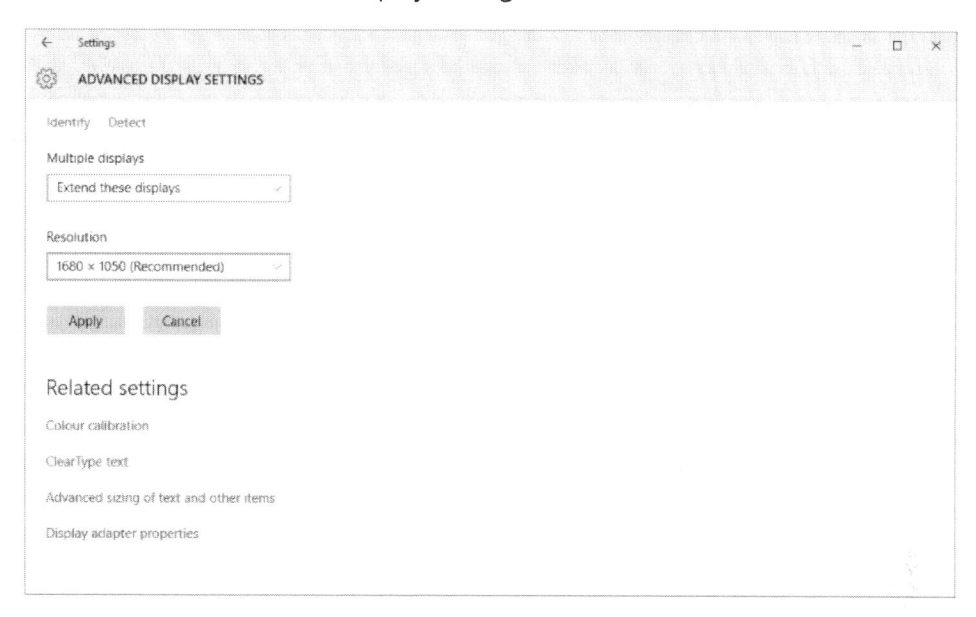

Figure 46.– Advanced display settings

You can now configure:

- **Colour calibration**. This is an advanced option and enables you to more accurately define colours on your display. This is probably only relevant to users working with files that must be accurately printed with the correct colours.

- **ClearType text**. ClearType text is enabled by default. It is a Microsoft software technology that has been in Windows for many versions and enables text to display better on LCD monitors.

Chapter 4 - Customizing Windows

- **Advanced sizing of text and other items**. For very high resolution monitors, items on the desktop and in desktop apps can appear very small. You can use the options here to control the size of these items. For smaller tablet displays, this should not be necessary.

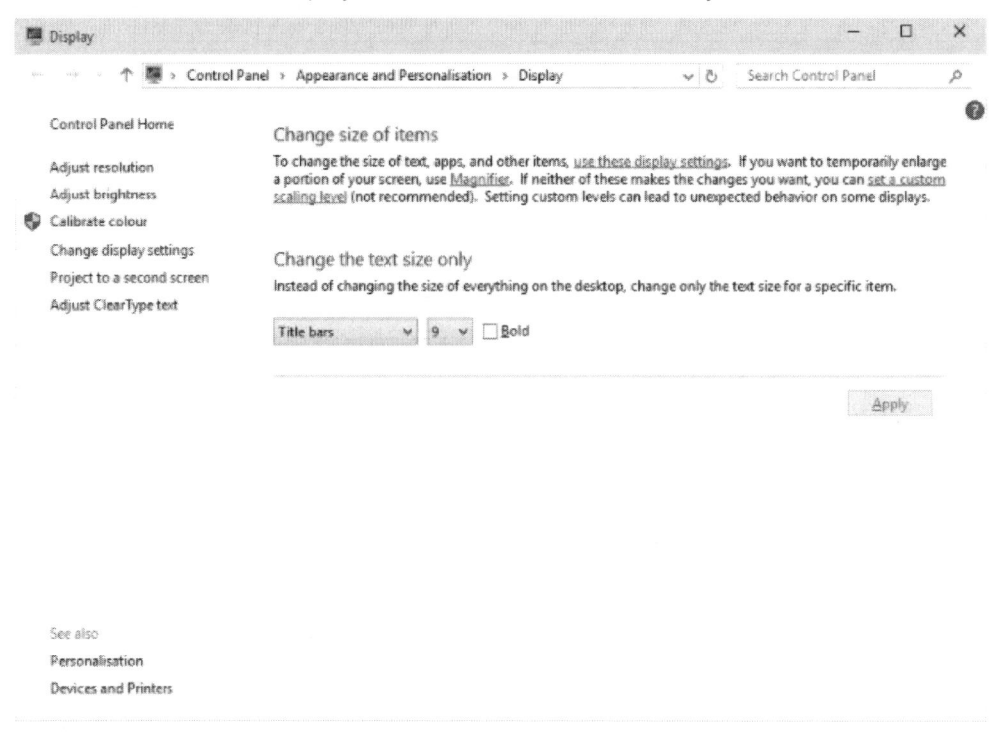

Figure 47.– Changing the size of desktop items

- **Display adapter properties**. Displays and enables you to configure the physical graphics adapter's properties, including advanced options such as its software driver and display modes. You should not need to make changes here.

Tablet Mode

Windows 10 is designed to run on a variety of device types, including both desktop computers without a touch screen and tablets with only a touch screen. This presents challenges for the Windows product team, tasked with devising a user interface that accommodates these different environments.

With Windows 8, Microsoft probably fell short of the mark, making the interface too touch-centric. Windows 8.1, a more significant release than the .1 might suggest, introduced some adjustments enabling users to use a Start button (removed in Windows 8) and also allowing users to choose whether to default to the Start screen or the desktop as their initial interface.

There was still some resistance in corporate environments to the improved Windows 8.1 interface. It was clear Microsoft had more work to do.

Note: When I started using Windows 8.1 on a tablet, I still struggled. I continued trying to use desktop apps instead of switching to Windows Store versions of the apps. So, for example, I used Microsoft Office Outlook® as my email program, and ended up trying to touch tiny little boxes in the app to reply to emails. But once I accepted I was using touch, and switched to using the built-in Mail app, life got a lot easier.

Windows 10 is a bit cleverer than Windows 8.1. It knows that its running on a tablet or on a desktop computer without touch, and it adjusts its settings accordingly. When the operating system is running on a tablet, tablet mode is enabled.

Note: It's even cleverer than that! When you use a convertible device, like a Surface tablet, if you fold the keyboard away (or detach it), Windows senses that and switches to Tablet mode. Fold it back, and it switches to Desktop mode.

Chapter 4 - Customizing Windows

This changes a number of behaviours within the operating system that make life a little easier for the user:

- **Start**. The Start screen displays full screen giving you more space for your groups of pinned apps.

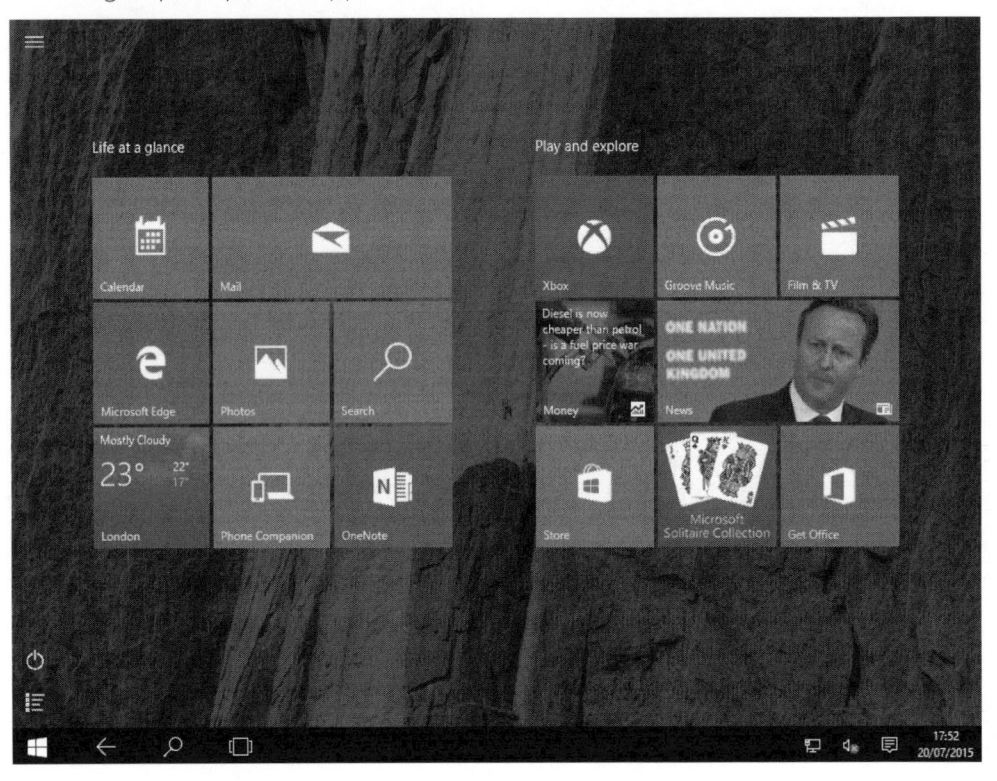

Figure 48.– Start in tablet mode

- **Apps**. Run full screen. You can swipe between them, or from the taskbar, use the **Task View** button to manage them.

Normally, you won't need to manually adjust from tablet mode to desktop mode, but to do so, open **Action Centre** by swiping left from the right of the screen. Touch the **Tablet mode** tile. The computer switches modes.

Chapter 4 - Customizing Windows

When in desktop mode, desktop shortcuts show on the desktop, and all apps (including Windows Store apps) run in windows on the desktop that you can move and resize like you did in earlier Windows versions.

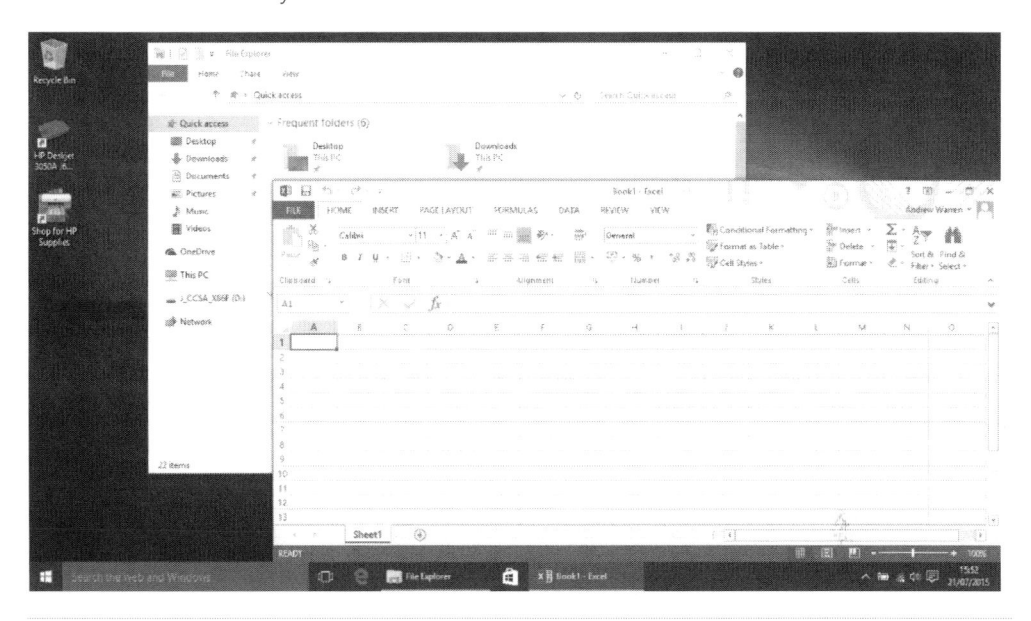

Figure 49.– Apps running in desktop mode

Chapter 4 - Customizing Windows

Action Centre

Action Centre brings together Notifications from the operating system, functions of the Action Centre from earlier versions of Windows, and also provides shortcut tiles to other important features of Windows. It's very similar to the notifications that you see in mobile phone operating systems.

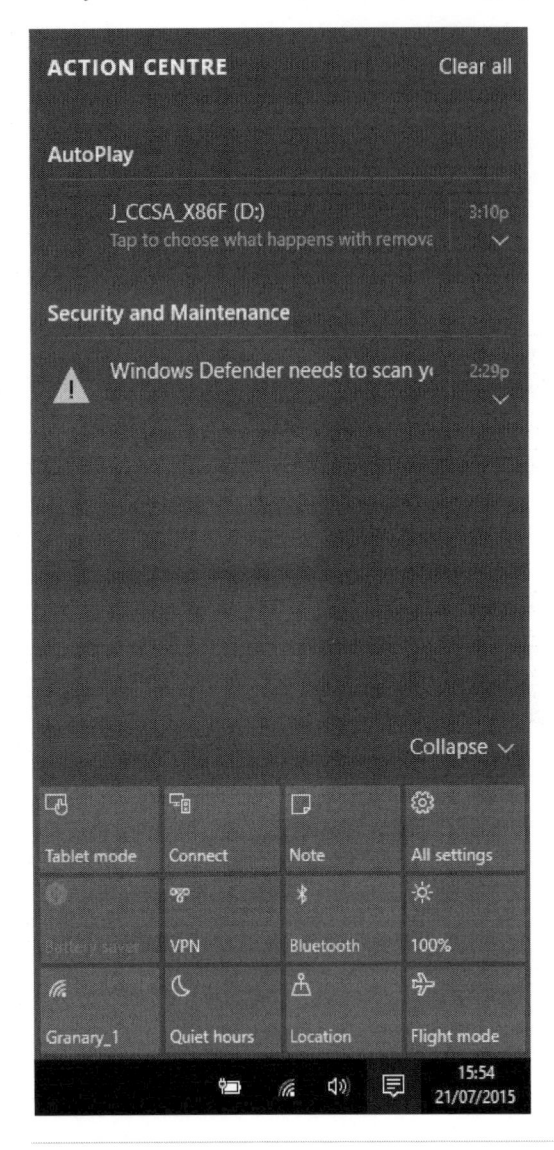

Figure 50.— Action Centre

Chapter 4 - Customizing Windows

The following are available from Action Centre:

- **Notifications**. These appear at the top of the Action Centre. When Windows wants to let you know about something, it raises a notification. You can see, and act upon, the notifications in a list. To respond to a notification, touch it. You can remove notifications by touching **Clear all** at the top of the page.

- **Tablet mode**. As discussed earlier, you can toggle between tablet and desktop modes.

- **Note**. Opens Microsoft OneNote.

- **Connect**. Enables you to find and connect to media servers. This includes Xbox and other devices running Windows that are sharing their media files. In can also include devices such as TV set top boxes.

- **All settings**. Provides a convenient shortcut to Settings.

- **Flight mode**. Disables all internal radios in the device including Wi-Fi and Bluetooth. This is handy when you want to save battery as well as when on an aircraft.

- **Battery saver**. Only available when your device is running on battery alone. Helps reduce power consumption. Battery saver can be configured in Settings.

- **Bluetooth**. Enables or disables the Bluetooth radio.

- **Location**. Enables or disables location services. Many services use location to customise services for your device; for example, mapping apps.

- **Rotation lock**. Enables or disables rotation lock. Normally, the display orientates itself based on the orientation of the physical device, switching between landscape and portrait modes. Use this option to lock the orientation irrespective of physical orientation.

- **VPN**. Launches Settings with the focus set on Network & Internet settings, with the VPN window active. A Virtual Private Network (VPN) is a special type of network that you can use to establish a secure connection to your workplace over the Internet. Usually, IT support staff configure these settings to match those required by your workplace network.

- **WiFi**. Enables or disables the Wi-Fi radio.

- **Quiet hours**. Toggles into quiet hours mode. This settings reduces the notifications you receive. Quiet hours can be configured in Settings.

Chapter 4 - Customizing Windows

- **Brightness**. Enables you to control display brightness. As the display is responsible for consuming a large percentage of the battery's power, it is important keep the brightness level as low as possible while still being visible in the ambient lighting conditions. Bear in mind that a display of 100% brightness is difficult to see when viewing the tablet in darkness.

Note: The options you have vary according to device type. For instance, Rotation lock is irrelevant for desktop devices, and does not display.

Determining what you are notified about

1. To configure what notifications you receive, open **Settings**.
2. Touch **System**.
3. Touch **Notifications & actions**.

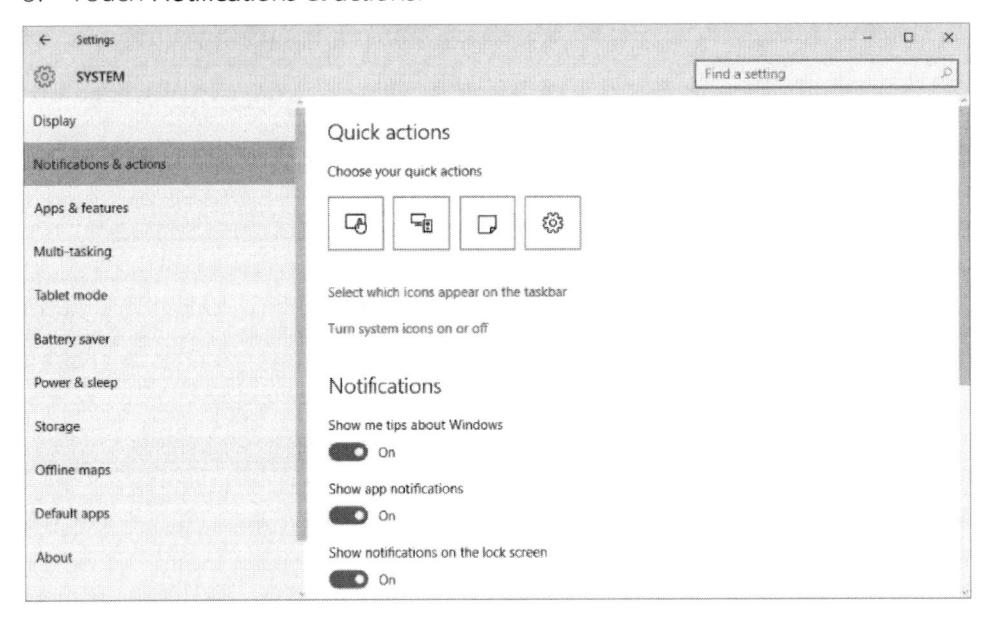

Figure 51.– Customizing Notifications

4. You can now select which icons will appear on the taskbar.

Note: Icons appear in the system tray area, to the far right of the taskbar.

Chapter 4 - Customizing Windows

5. Touch **Select which icons appear on the taskbar** and then select which apps should appear, including whether you want the **Network**, **Volume**, and **Microsoft OneDrive** icons to appear. Touch back.

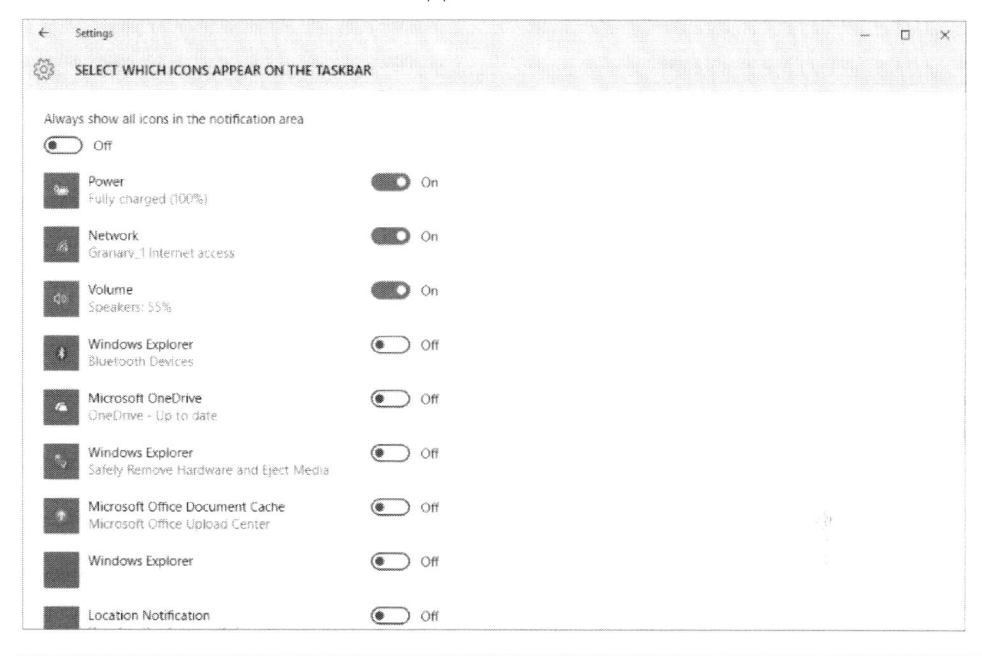

Figure 52.– Configuring which icons appear on the taskbar

6. Touch **Turn system icons on or off**. Then choose which icons you want. Touch back.

Figure 53.– Turning system icons on or off

7. Under **Notifications**, you can:
   - Show me tips about Windows
   - Show app notifications

Note: For some specific apps, you can enable or disable notifications individually.

   - Show notifications on the lock screen
   - Show alarms, reminders and incoming VOIP calls on the lock screen
   - Hide notifications when presenting (on by default)

8. Close Settings.

Chapter 5

Working with Apps

What you will do in this chapter:

- Configure Mail, People, and Calendar apps
- Install Windows Store Apps
- Install desktop apps
- Switch between running apps

Chapter 5 - Working with Apps

Configuring Mail, People, and Calendar

The built-in **Mail**, **People**, and **Calendar** apps are linked, which makes sense when you think about it. After all, the desktop app, Office Outlook, combines these elements. So, it probably makes sense to try to use an email provider that can offer you contact management, email, and schedule management.

Although I have an email account with a bespoke service provider, linked to my own domain name, I use an Outlook.com account to retrieve my mail[19]. This is because Outlook.com offers push synchronization.

Note: Push sync enables the email provider to send you updates to your devices, rather than you having to remember to retrieve items.

The other advantage of using Outlook.com within the Microsoft ecosystem is that the account can potentially be the same as the Microsoft account name you use to sign in with; this makes it very easy to configure the account. It also has the advantage of you only having to remember one thing.

For the following procedures, I have assumed you have an Outlook.com email account. If you do not, you must substitute the appropriate settings within the account properties for these apps.

Note: To get an Outlook.com account, visit the following website and sign in with your Microsoft account. Then create an Outlook.com alias for your account.
http://www.microsoft.com/en-us/outlook-com/

---

[19] *I created a rule at my ISP to forward all mail to my Outlook.com mailbox.*

Configuring Mail

Adding an Outlook.com account

To configure the mail account to use Outlook.com:

1. From Start, touch **Mail**.
2. Touch **Get Started**.
3. The Mail app displays your Microsoft account. If this is also your email account, then touch **Ready to go** and proceed to **Configuring Mail options** further down this lesson.
4. Otherwise, on the **Accounts** page, touch **Add account** and then touch **Done**.

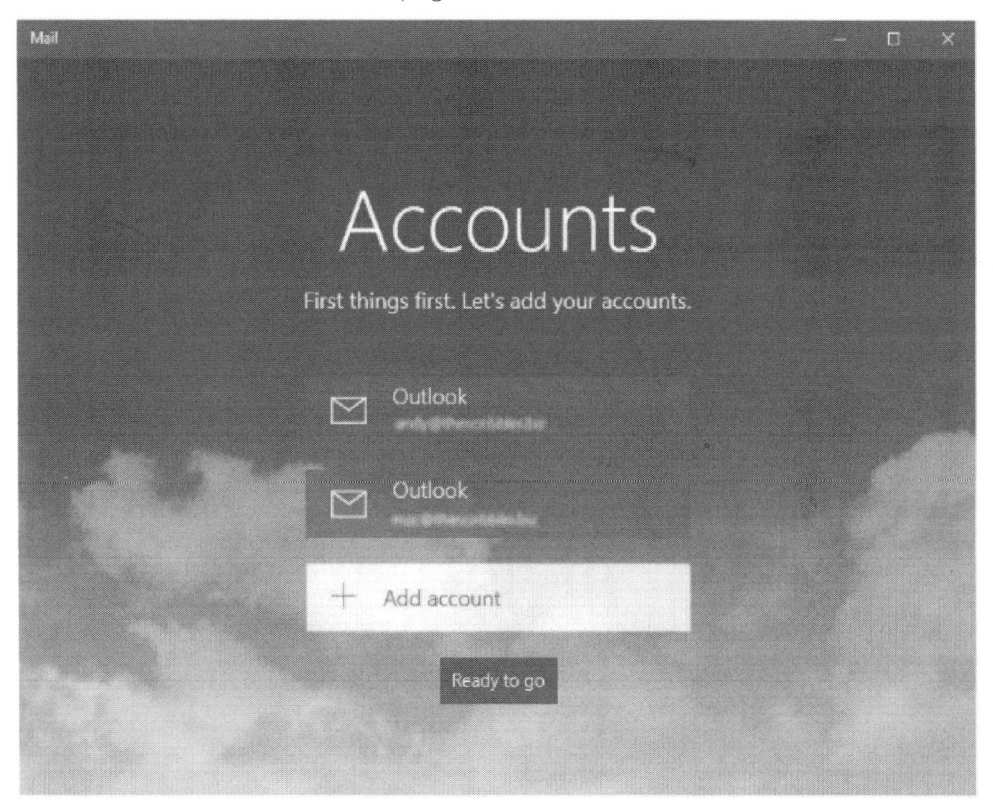

Figure 54.– Add an account

5. In the **Choose an account** window, touch the account type which most closely matches the one you have.

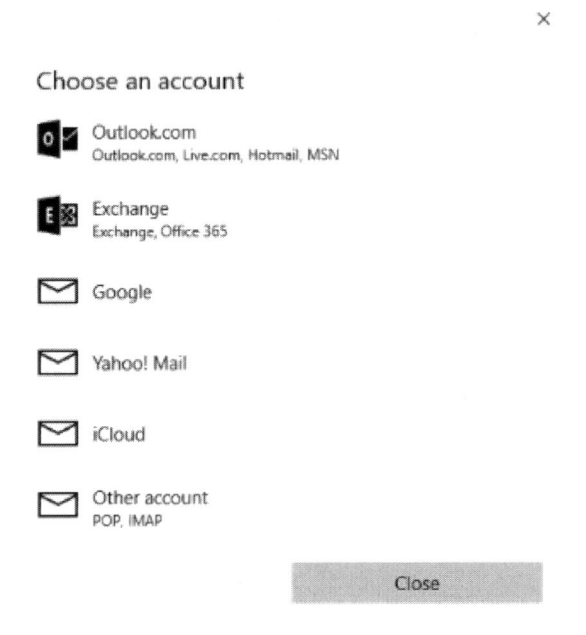

```
Choose an account

    Outlook.com
    Outlook.com, Live.com, Hotmail, MSN

    Exchange
    Exchange, Office 365

    Google

    Yahoo! Mail

    iCloud

    Other account
    POP, IMAP

              Close
```

Figure 55.– Choosing the type of email account

6. If you have an Outlook.com account, touch **Outlook.com**. If you are using a work-based email account on Exchange Server, then touch **Exchange**. Gmail users should touch **Google**. If you have a POP or IMAP account, touch **Other account**. The precise steps that follow vary depending upon the option selected.

Note: If necessary, you may have to touch **Other account** and manually enter the required information. You'll need to know the names of the servers your service provider uses to provide email. You'll also need to know what type of email server it is; for example, POP3, IMAP4, or HTTP. Again, your ISP should provide all the information you need. See below for more information.

Chapter 5 - Working with Apps

7. Enter your Microsoft account details and touch **Sign in**.

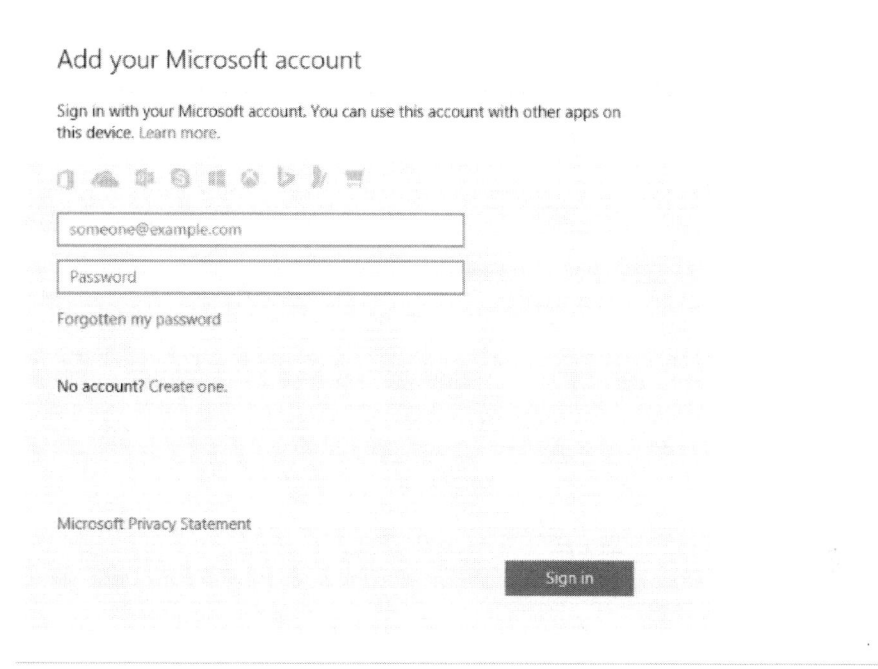

Figure 56.– Sign in with your Microsoft account

8. If all is successful, at the **All done!** page, touch **Done**.

Chapter 5 - Working with Apps

9. You are returned to the **Accounts** page. Your new account is listed. Touch **Ready to go**.

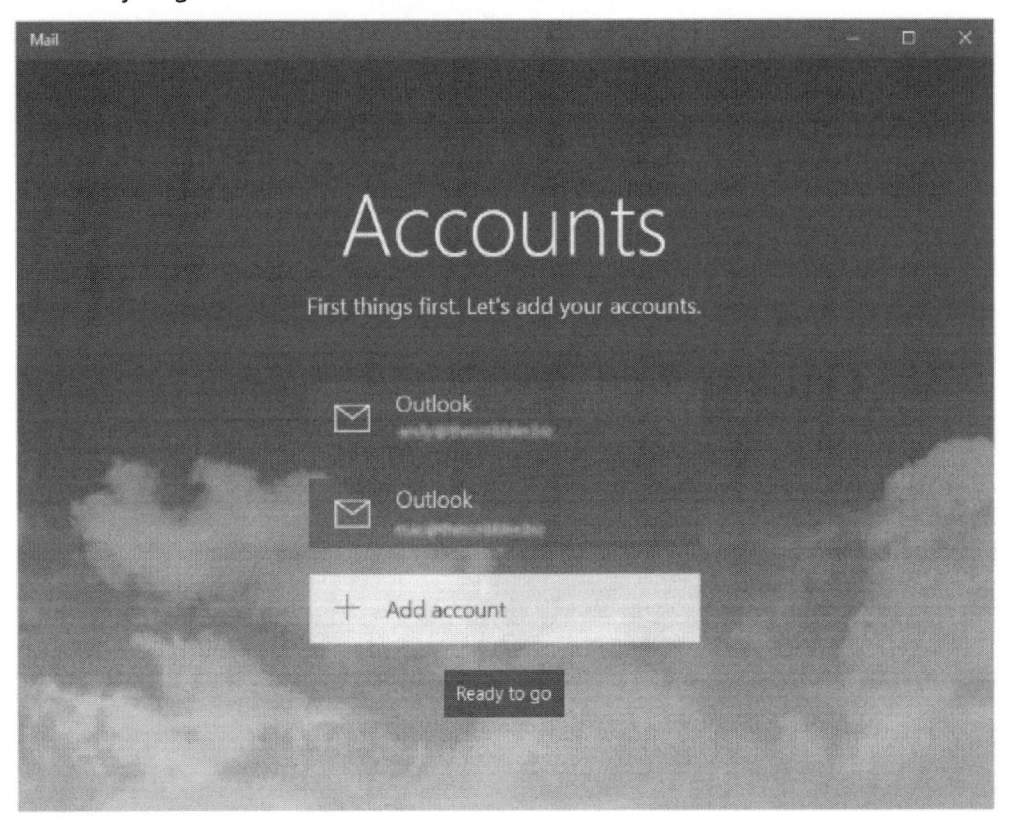

Figure 57.– You are ready to go

Chapter 5 - Working with Apps

10. Your inbox opens.

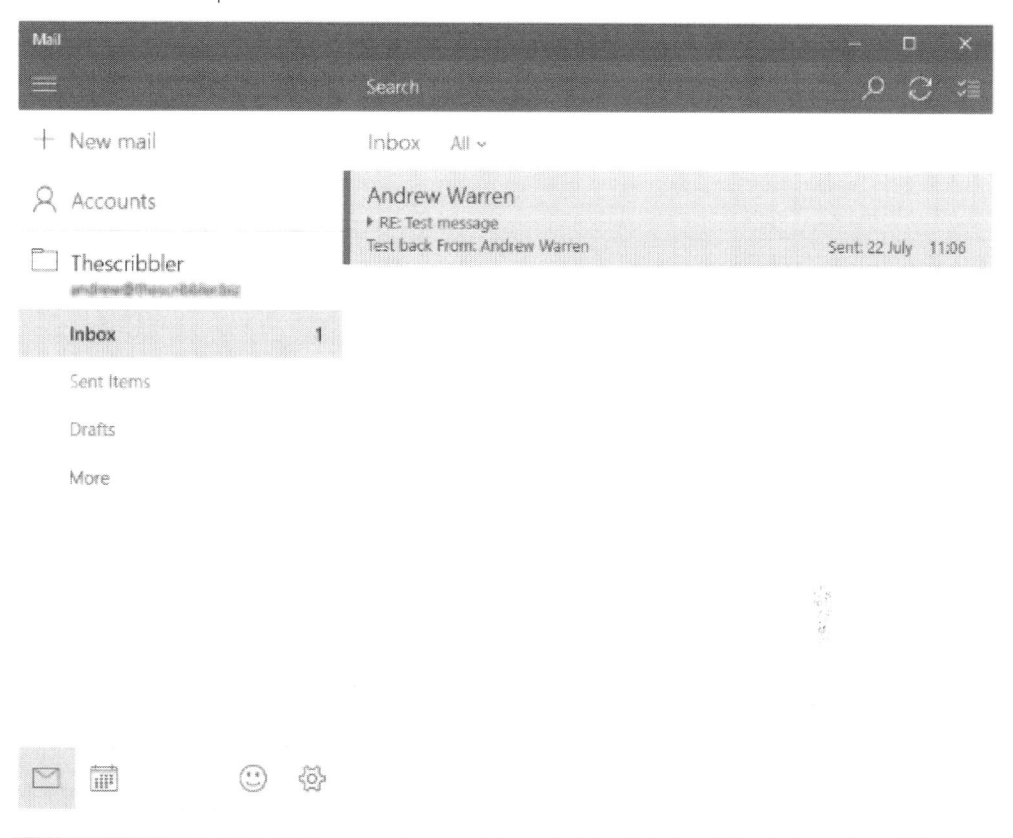

Figure 58.– Your Outlook.com inbox

Note: If you must add another account later, from within Mail, touch **Options** and then touch **Settings**. Touch **Account** and you can go through the process of adding a new account.

Chapter 5 - Working with Apps

Configuring Mail options

Once your email account is configured, in tablet mode, you can configure options by swiping in from the right and touching **Options**. You can then configure a background picture, determine what will happen when you swipe right / hover and swipe left / hover over items, configure an email signature to be appended to each message, enable or disable email notifications, and, when necessary, enable logging.

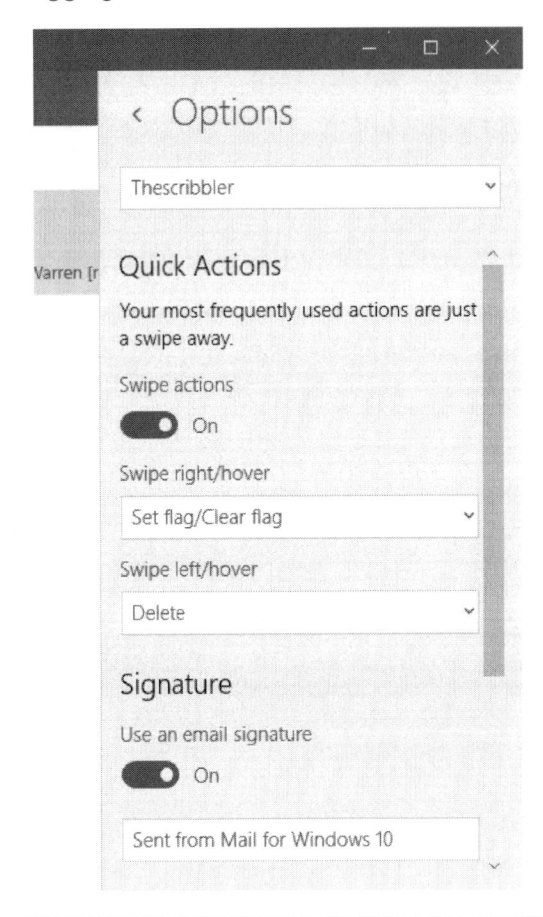

Figure 59.– Mail options

Chapter 5 - Working with Apps

Configuring Calendar

If you are using an Outlook.com email account, you already have calendar and contacts. It's now just a question of configuring the Windows apps to use them. From within Mail, touch the **Calendar** symbol on the left – or else touch **Calendar** in Start.

1. In the setup wizard, touch **Get Started**.
2. Your Outlook.com email account should be listed. Touch **Ready to go**. Your calendar displays.

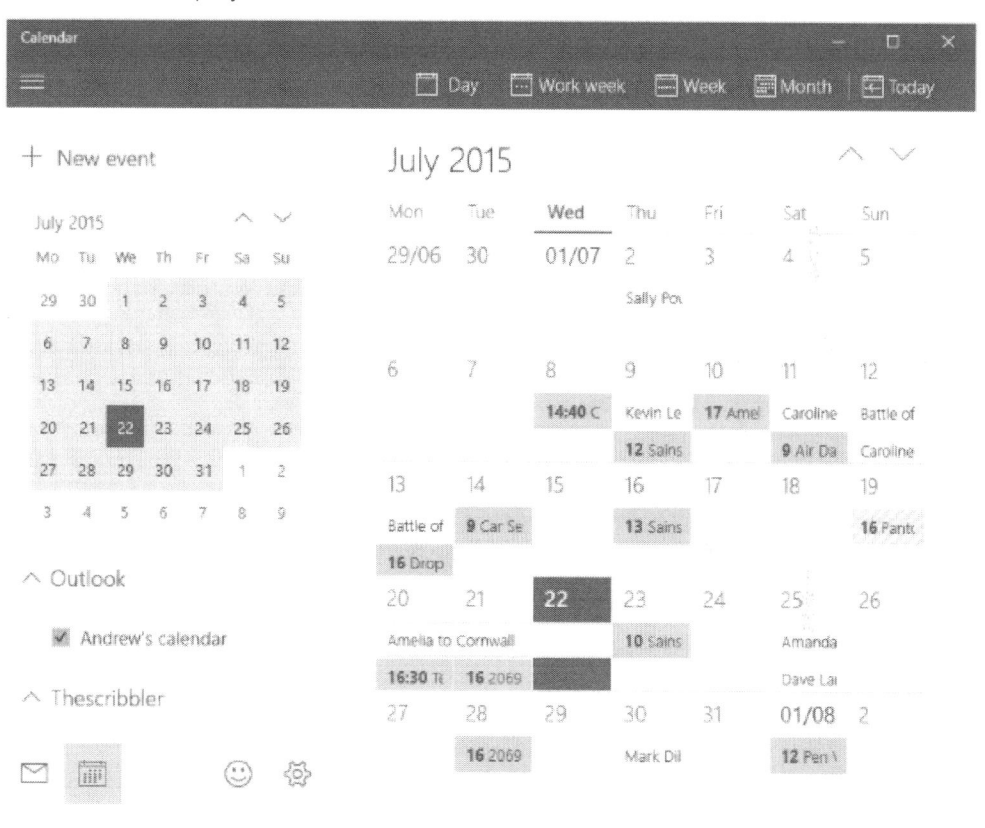

Figure 60.– Outlook.com calendar

Chapter 5 - Working with Apps

Configure Calendar options

To configure Calendar options, swipe right from the left and touch **Calendar Settings**. You can configure:

- **First Day of the Week**. Defaults to Monday.
- **Days in Work Week**. Defaults to Monday through Friday.
- **Working Hours**. Defaults to 8am to 5pm.

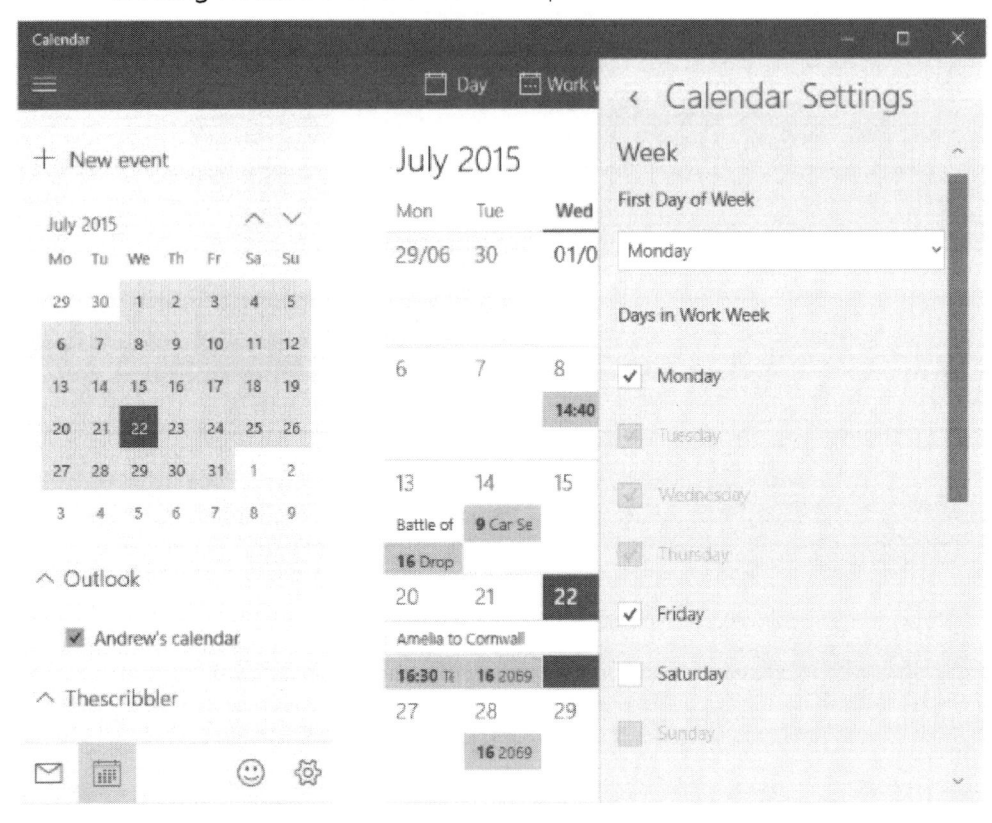

Figure 61.– Calendar settings

Configuring People

Outlook.com also provides you with synchronized contacts. To access your contacts, you can, of course, simply create a new email and start to type recipients' names. Your contacts are displayed as a context sensitive list below your **To:** box.

To work directly with your contacts, from Start, touch **People**. Your list of contacts opens. You can then configure your contacts.

Note: If you use Windows Phone, you can sync your contacts from your phone to Outlook.com and these will then sync to all your other Windows devices.

Installing Windows Store Apps

In the last few years, the way users have worked with their devices has been changed by the proliferation of small, focused apps that are made available online in managed portals such as the Google Play Store and the Apple App store. One of the great things about Windows 10 is the ability to install similar apps from the Windows Store.

Note: Because the apps are deployed from the Windows Store, you can rest assured that the app does not contain malicious code.

To install apps from the Windows Store, you must be signed in to your device using a Microsoft account. If you intend to install apps for which there is a charge (many apps in the Windows Store are free), then you must also provide payment information that is stored securely in your Microsoft account.

Installing an app

To install an app from the Windows Store, use the following procedure:

1. Sign in using your Microsoft account.
2. Switch to **Start**.
3. Touch **Store**.

Figure 62.– Accessing the Store

4. In the Windows Store app, browse for the app you want. In this case, we're going to install the Facebook app. In the **Search** box, type **Facebook** and touch **Search**.
5. In the results list, touch **Facebook**.

Note: Many apps are free, some are free for a trial period, and some apps require payment either at installation, or by in-app purchases.

6. Touch **Install** to launch the app installer. The app starts to install.

Chapter 5 - Working with Apps

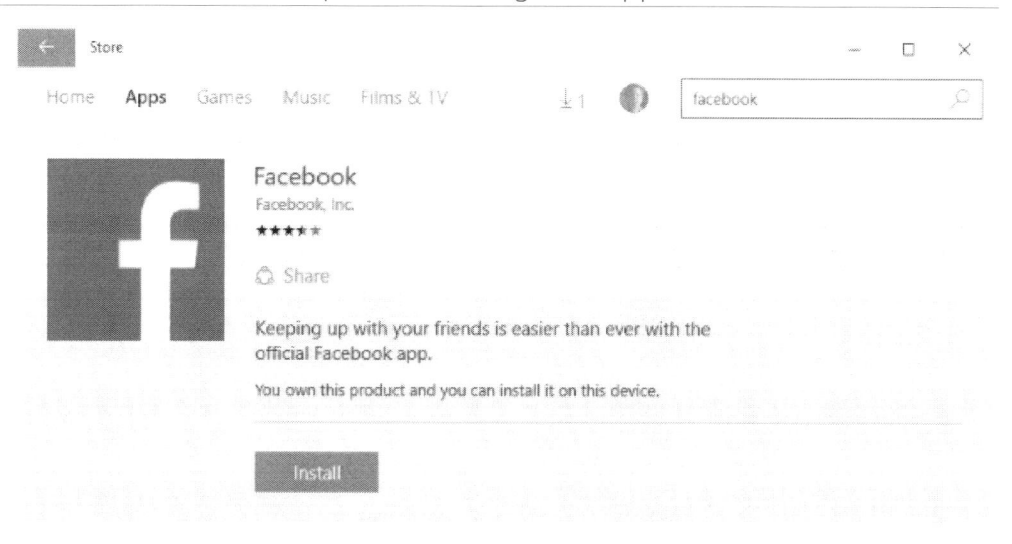

Figure 63.– Installing your app

7. Switch back to **Start** when the app is installed.

8. Your new app is shown in the **All apps** list, highlighted with **New**.

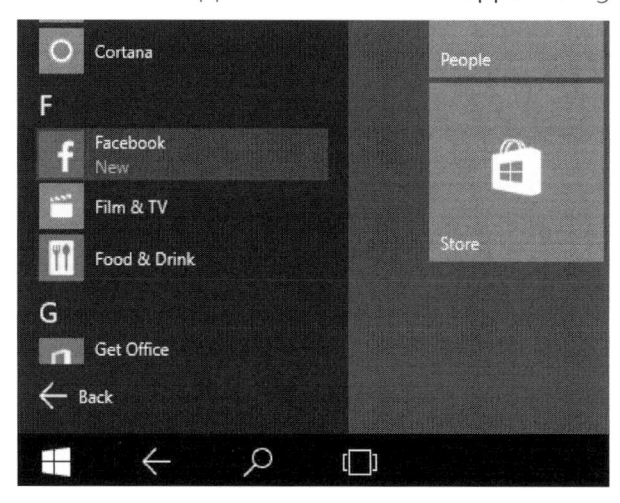

Figure 64.– Your new app

9. To add your app to a group, pin it to Start. Touch and hold your app, and then touch **Pin to Start**. You can then drag the app to an appropriate Start group as described earlier in this book.

Chapter 5 - Working with Apps

Managing your apps

From time to time, you may want to update or delete your apps.

Uninstalling an app

1. If you no longer want an app, then from the Start screen, touch and hold the app you want to remove and then touch **Uninstall**.

2. At the confirmation window, touch **Uninstall**.

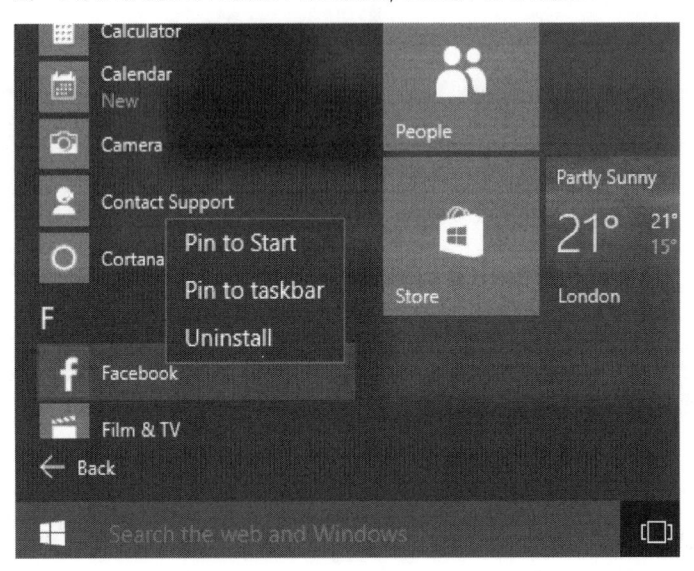

Figure 65.– Uninstalling an app

Note: Although the app is uninstalled from this device, it remains on any other of your devices where you installed it.

Chapter 5 - Working with Apps

Viewing your installed apps

1. To view your installed apps, from **Store**, touch the head and shoulders icon in the menu bar, and then touch **Downloads**.

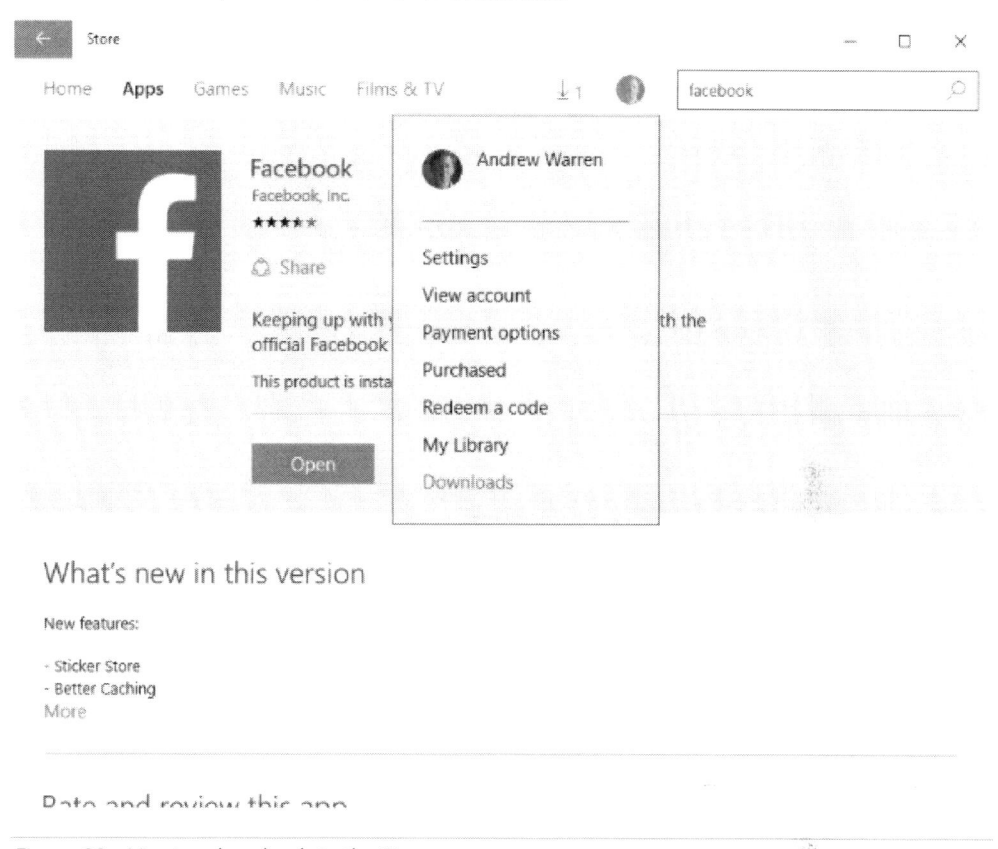

Figure 66.– Viewing downloads in the Store

Chapter 5 - Working with Apps

2. In the **Downloads and installs** list, you can see your apps. Some of these are built-in apps, others have been installed by you.

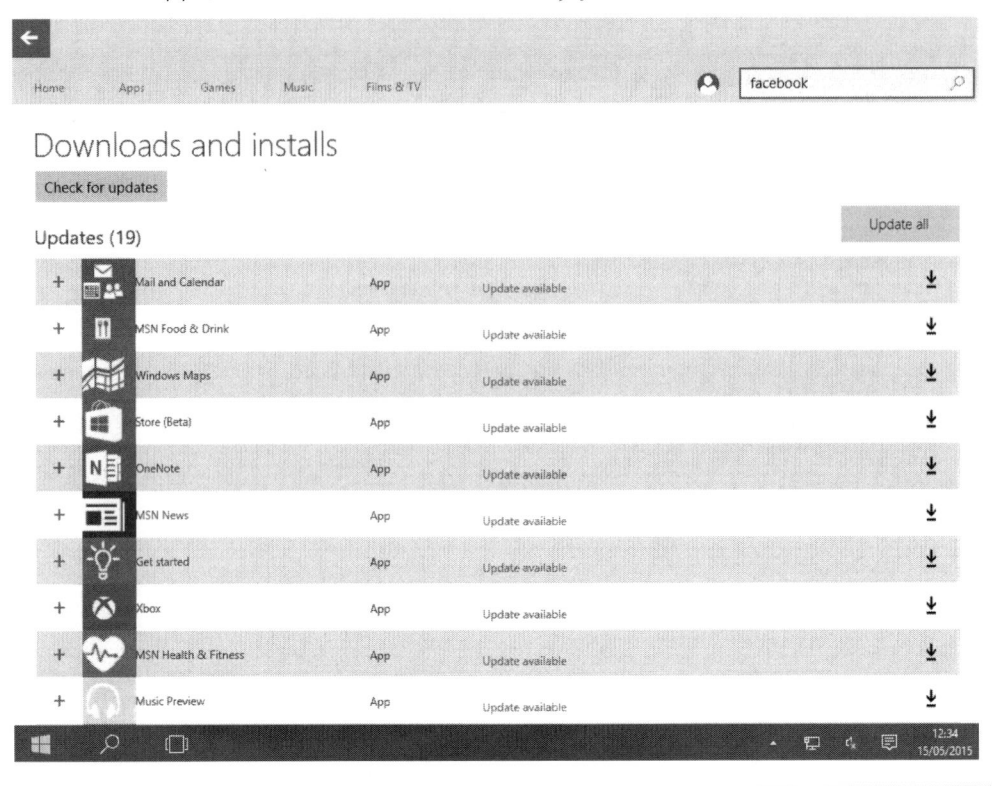

Figure 67.– Viewing downloads in the Store

Chapter 5 - Working with Apps

You can view installed app updates from Settings, too.

1. To view App update settings, open **Settings**.
2. Touch **System**.
3. Touch **Apps & features**.

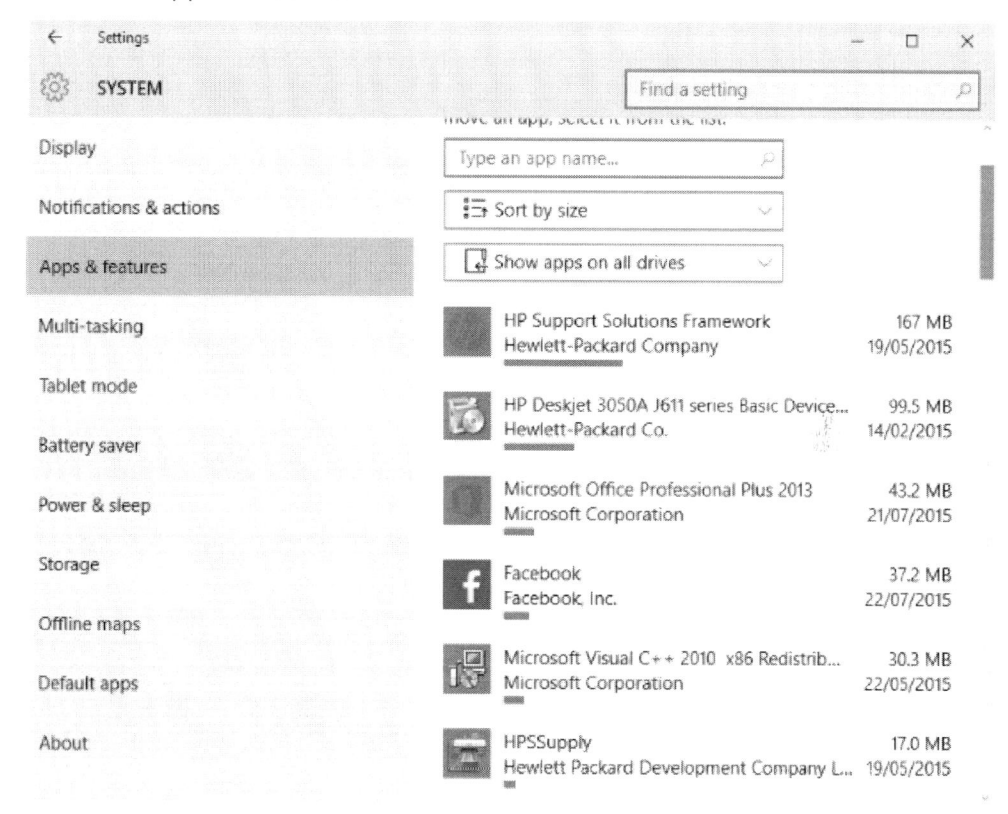

Figure 68.– Viewing installed apps from Settings

Chapter 5 - Working with Apps

4. To remove an app, touch the app, and then touch **Uninstall**.

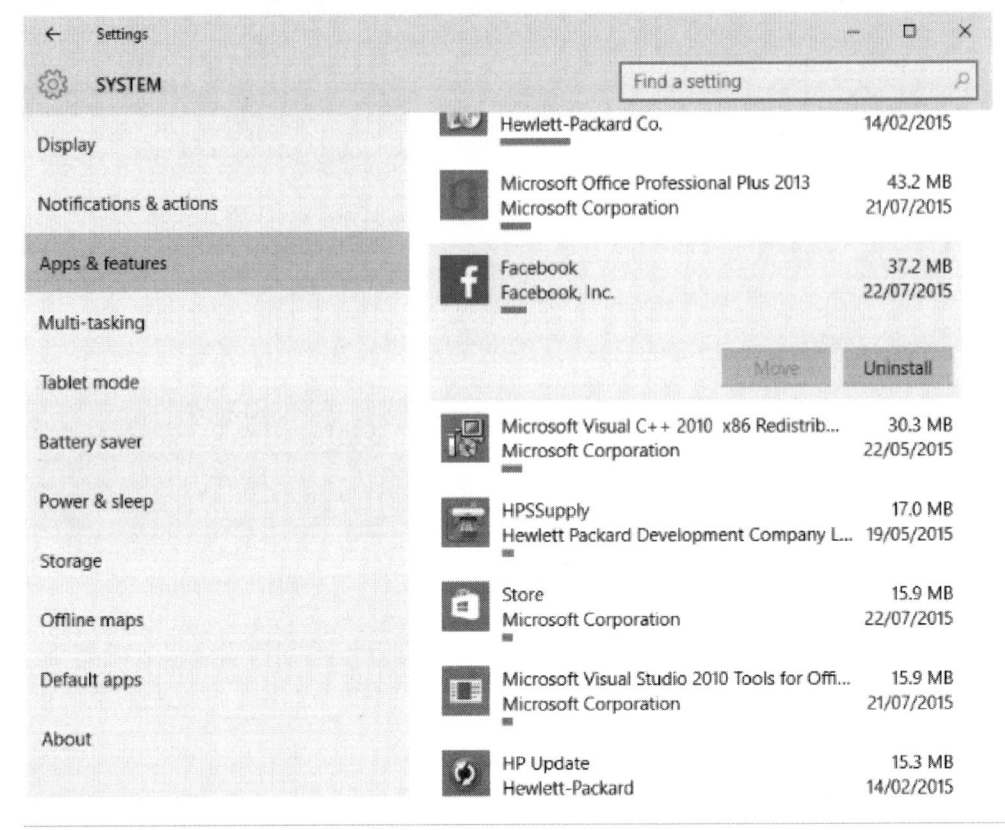

Figure 69.– Uninstall apps from Settings

Chapter 5 - Working with Apps

Updating your apps

To update your apps, from the Store app, you can view the **Download** apps list (see above) and then determine which ones require updating.

1. To check for updates, touch **Check for updates**.
2. You can update your apps, either singly or all at the same time. To update all apps, touch **Update all**.
3. To update a single app, touch the **Download** link to the right of the app. The app will move to the bottom of the list as it is updated.

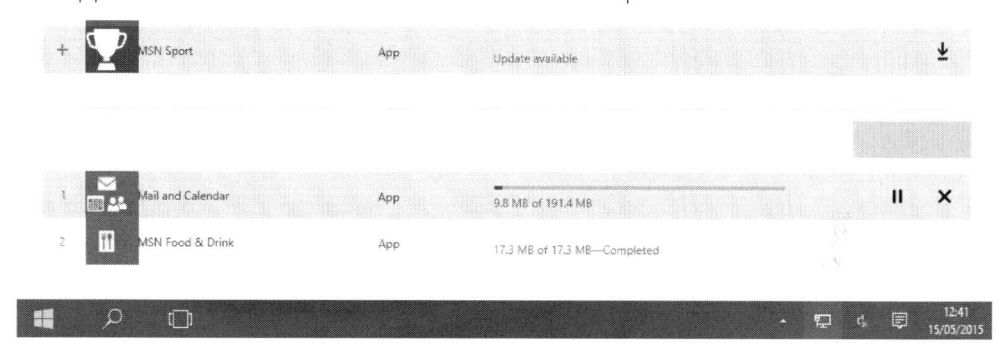

Figure 70.– Apps updating

Chapter 5 - Working with Apps

To configure automatic app updates:

1. To view your installed apps, from **Store**, touch the head and shoulders icon in the menu bar, and then touch **Settings**.

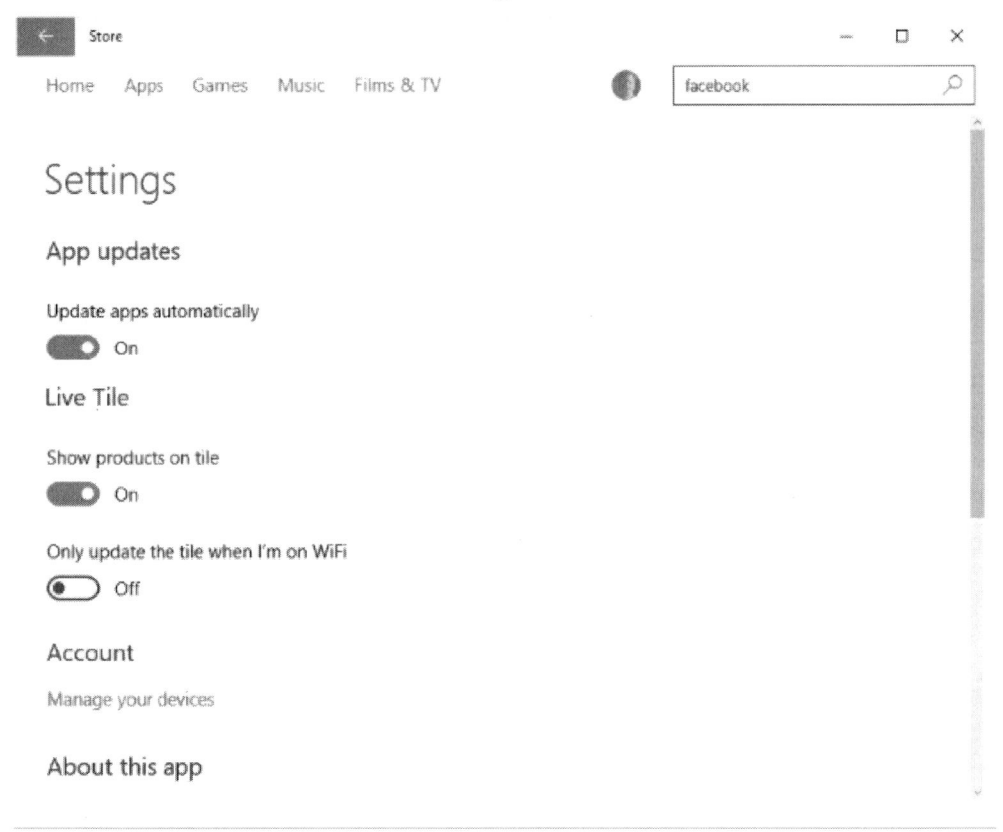

Figure 71.– Enable automatic app updates

2. Turn on **Update apps automatically**.

Installing Desktop Apps

The process of installing desktop apps has not changed significantly in Windows 10. Generally, you must obtain a product DVD or download[20] the software that you wish to install.

Note: In Windows 10, some vendors are making their desktop apps available from the Store. This will make it easier for you to install and maintain your apps.

You can then launch the installation program from the download or product DVD. The installation program is often called Setup.exe, but you must consult your software vendor's documentation for full details.

Note: Some devices with Windows 10 also come with a full or time-limited license for the use of Office 365. For more information about Office 365, visit:
https://products.office.com/en-gb/office-365-home

32-bit or 64-bit

Some desktop apps, such as Microsoft Office 2013, are available in both 32-bit and 64-bit variants. If your device is installed with a 64-bit version of Windows 10, then obtain and install the 64-bit version of your app. You can run 32-bit apps on a 64-bit version of Windows 10, but you cannot install and run a 64-bit version of an app on 32-bit versions of Windows 10.

Installing Office 2013

To demonstrate the process of installing a desktop app, the following steps are those required to install Microsoft Office Professional 2013.

1. Insert the Microsoft Office 2013 product DVD in your device.

Note: If you do not have a DVD drive (because your device is a tablet), then you can download an ISO of the DVD. Double-tap the ISO file in File Explorer to mount the file as if it was a DVD.

2. Windows prompts you what to do when you insert a DVD. Touch the **Tap to choose what happens with this disc** prompt to configure the action.

---

[20] *As you are downloading software from a potentially untrusted source rather than the tightly controlled Windows Store, it is important to exercise caution as downloaded software is often a common source of malicious code. Ensure that you have an antivirus and anti-malware software program installed on your device, such as Windows Defender. This can help to protect you against malicious code downloads.*

Chapter 5 - Working with Apps

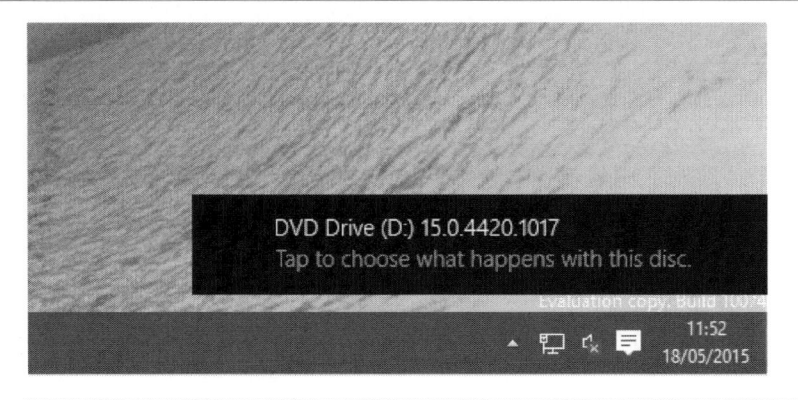

Figure 72.– Inserting a product DVD

Note: You can configure this behaviour when prompted the first time. You can also change this through Settings.

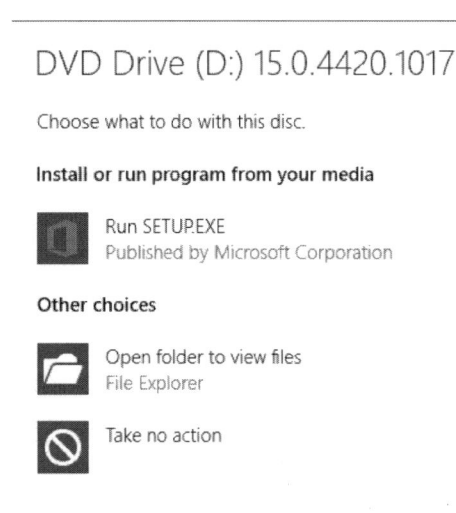

Figure 73.– Configuring autorun

3. In the **Choose what to do with this disc** window, touch **Run SETUP.EXE**.

Note: If the installation program does not automatically run when you insert the product DVD, then use File Explorer to navigate to the DVD drive and locate the **Setup.exe** (or similar) program and launch it.

Chapter 5 - Working with Apps

4. You are prompted by **User Account Control** to confirm that you want to run the Setup program. This security feature helps to protect your device against malicious software and unintended or unwanted configuration changes. Since you know this software is safe, and you intended to run the program, touch **Yes**.

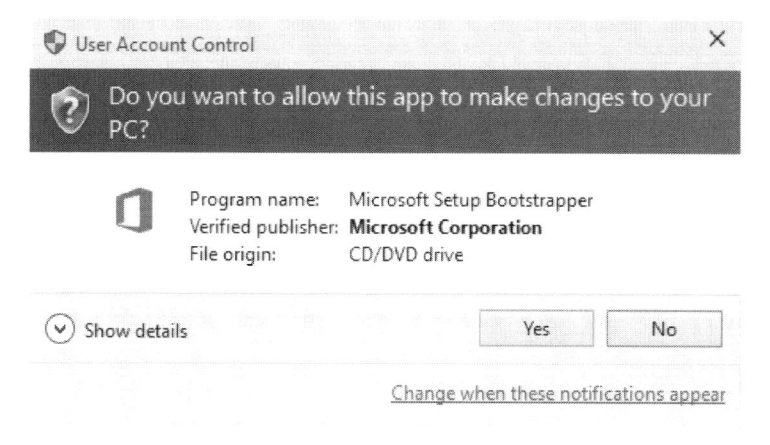

Figure 74.– User Account Control prompt

5. Most desktop software has defined terms of use. These must be displayed by the software vendor during the installation. Typically, you will see a prompt to which you must agree to continue. Touch **I accept the terms of this agreement** and then touch **Continue**.

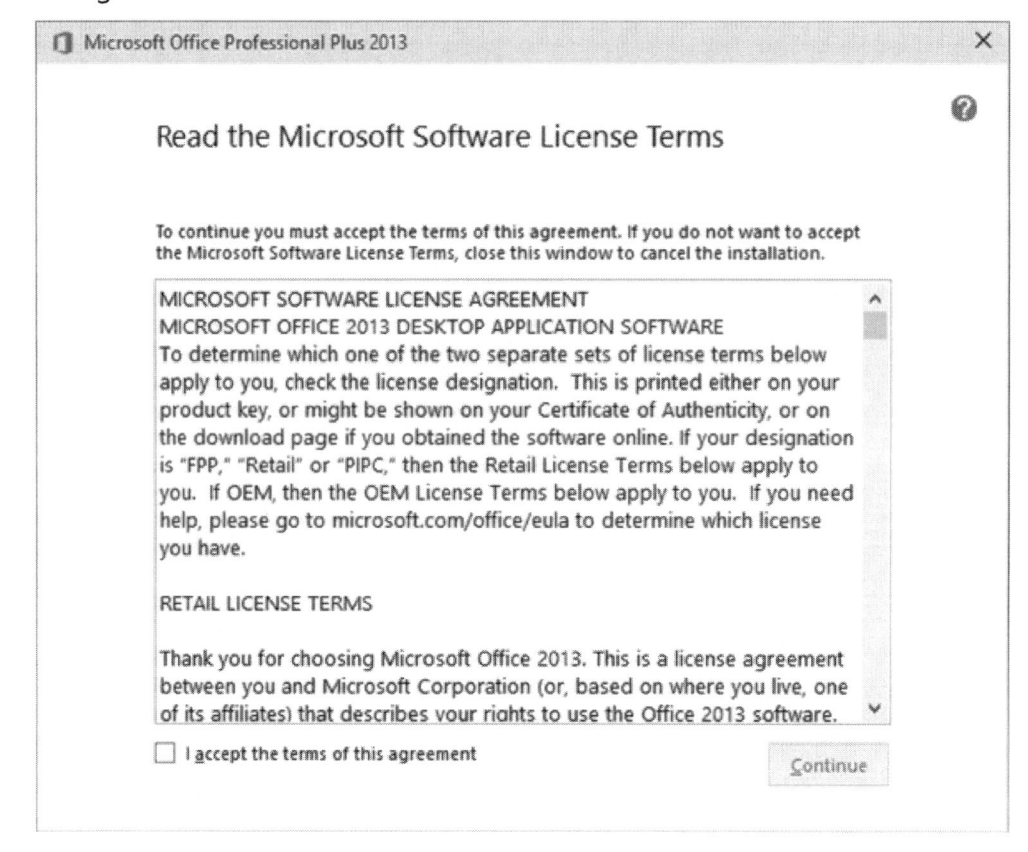

Figure 75.– Licensing terms

6. You are now prompted to customize the installation by determining which components of Office you want to install. Touch **Customize**.

Note: Be especially careful at this point with free, downloaded apps. You are often prompted to choose between a Typical / Standard install or a Custom install. Typical installs often result in additional, unwanted components being downloaded and installed on your device, and also to changes being made to your web browser homepage. Always choose Custom and then clear any check boxes that appear subsequently that relate to additional software components or configuration changes that you don't want.

Chapter 5 - Working with Apps

7. For each component displayed, touch the down arrow and then select whether the component will be available or not. When you have configured the components you want, touch **Install Now**.

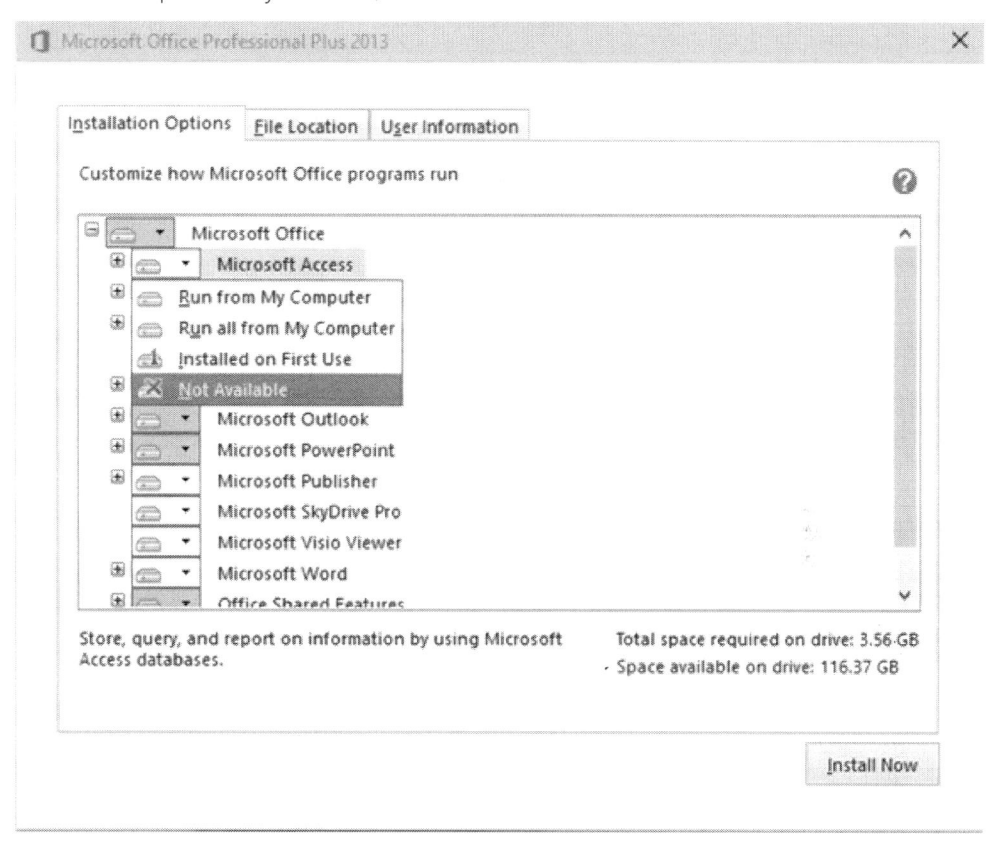

Figure 76.– Customize the components you want to install

Note: You can add or remove components later from Settings.

8. The installation of the app proceeds. When prompted, touch **Close**. You can remove the product DVD, or remove the mounted ISO from File Explorer (touch and hold the drive and then touch **Eject**).

Chapter 5 - Working with Apps

9. Switch to **Start**. Your Office apps are available in All apps. You can pin the apps that you use frequently to the Start screen as described earlier in this book.

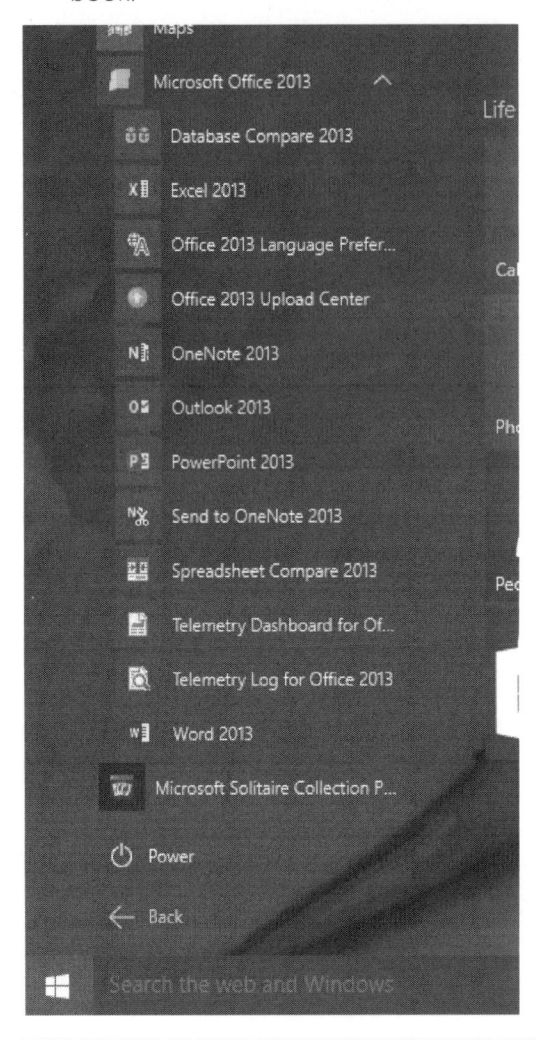

Figure 77.– Microsoft Office apps list in Start

Syncing desktop apps

A final thought about desktop apps. These apps do not synchronize between your devices. If you want to have Office Word available on all your Windows devices, you must install it on each device.

Note: You may require additional software licenses to install the app on multiple devices.

Activation

Microsoft Office must be activated. On first use, and subsequently, you are prompted to Activate Office. Activation proves that you have a valid, licensed copy of the software. When you see this prompt, you must enter a product key by touching **Enter a product key instead**.

Enter the product key that you have, and touch **Continue**. If you have an Internet connection, your key is validated, and Office is activated.

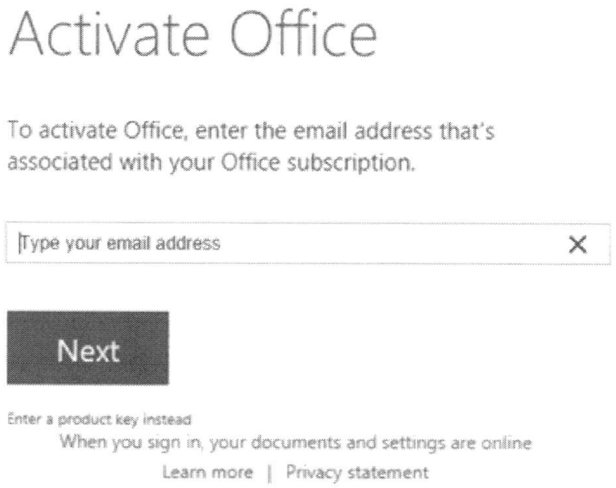

Figure 78.– Activation

Chapter 5 - Working with Apps

User Account Control

A note about security. User Account Control (UAC) is a security feature that Microsoft introduced in Windows Vista. As much malicious software, including computer viruses, are introduced inadvertently by users installing apps, UAC is designed to prompt users when they perform tasks that require elevated privileges. These elevated privileges are required when desktop apps are installed and when significant configuration changes are attempted on your device.

You can configure how UAC prompts you, and it is also possible to disable UAC – although that is not recommended. To configure UAC:

1. From Start, in the **Search the web and windows** box, type **Control Panel**.
2. At the top of the returned apps list, touch **Control Panel**.

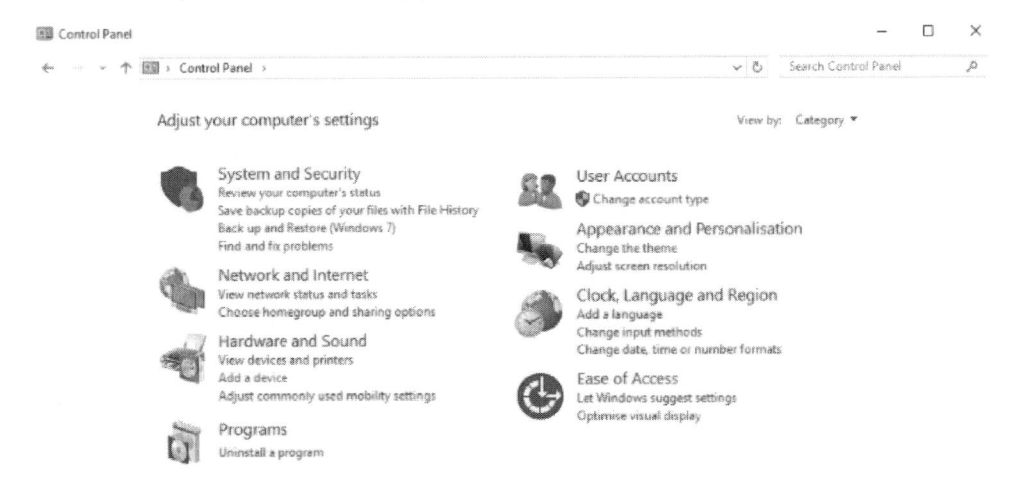

Figure 79.– Control Panel

Chapter 5 - Working with Apps

3. In Control Panel, touch **System and Security** and then touch **Change User Account Control settings**.

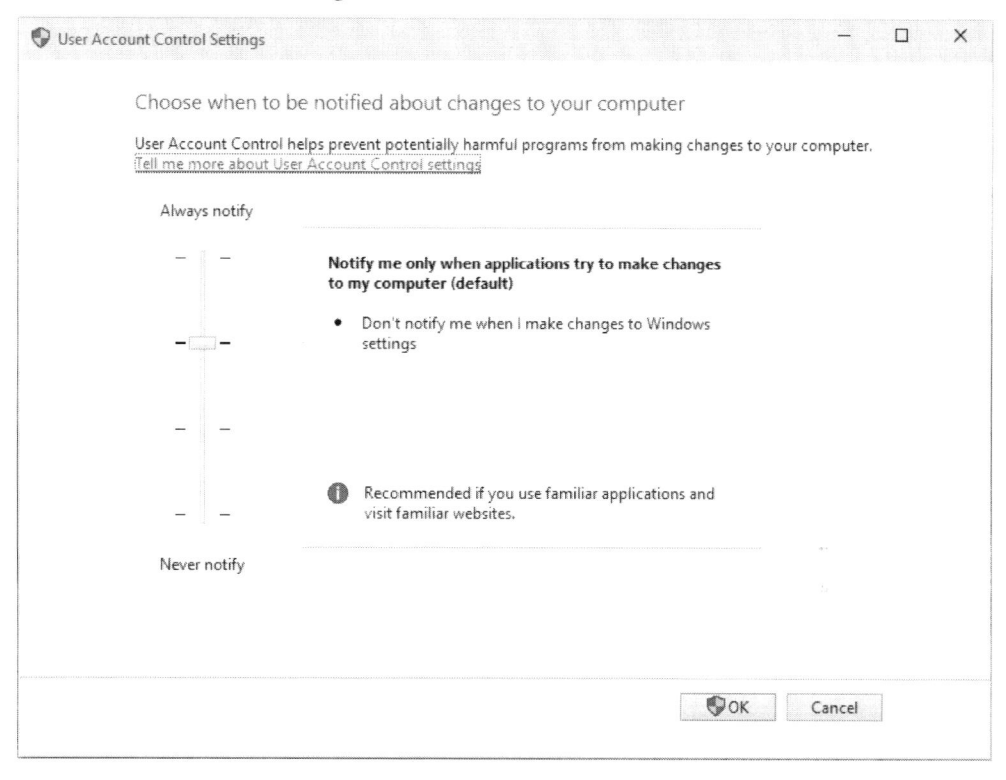

Figure 80.– User Account Control settings

4. Use the slider bar to adjust the settings. Sliding to the bottom disables UAC – not recommended. Sliding to the top makes UAC more intrusive, but your device more secure. Typically, you will not adjust these settings.

5. When you are happy with the UAC level, touch **OK**.

Chapter 5 - Working with Apps

Switching Between Apps

In tablet mode, when you are running multiple apps, you can switch between them by swiping from the left. This displays all running apps, both desktop apps and Windows Store apps. You can touch whichever app you want to make full screen.

The **Task View** button (shown to the right of the Search button) on the taskbar, enables you to view running apps without swiping.

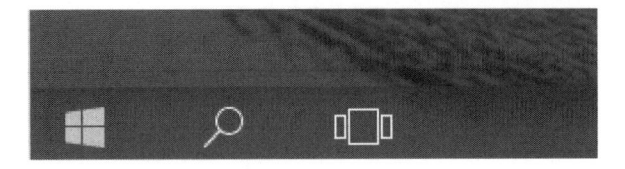

Figure 81.– Task View button

In Desktop mode, use the **Task View** button to view running apps.

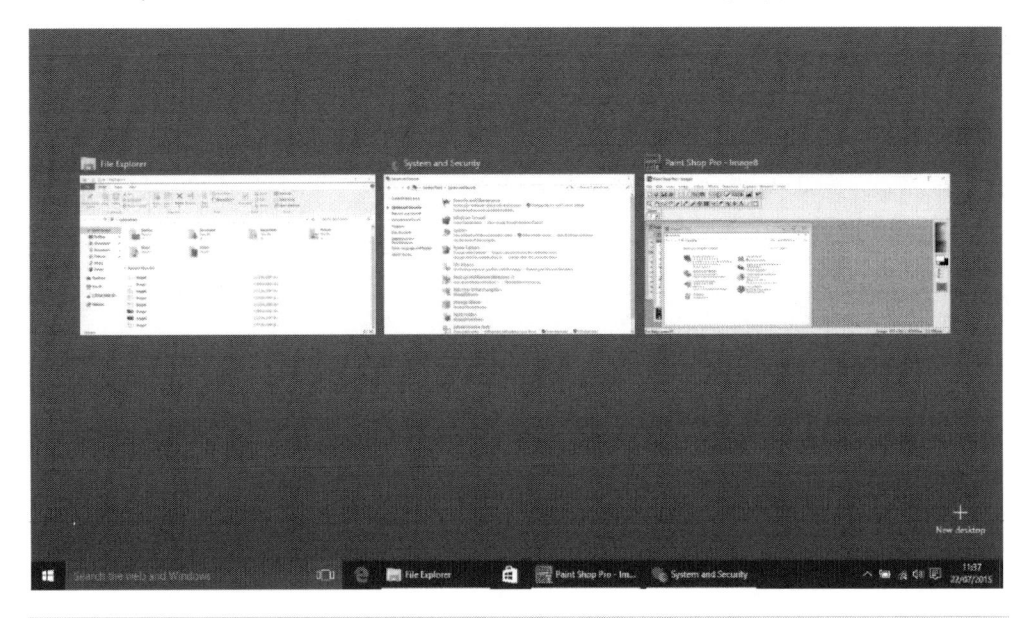

Figure 82.– Viewing running apps in desktop mode

Note: The **New desktop** button (far right of the display), enables you to organize your apps into virtual desktops. If you close a desktop, the apps running within it are attached to the remaining desktop.

Page - 100

Chapter 5 - Working with Apps

In Desktop mode, you can resize and drag and drop apps just as you did in earlier Windows versions. You can also run them full screen by touching the maximize button for the desired app.

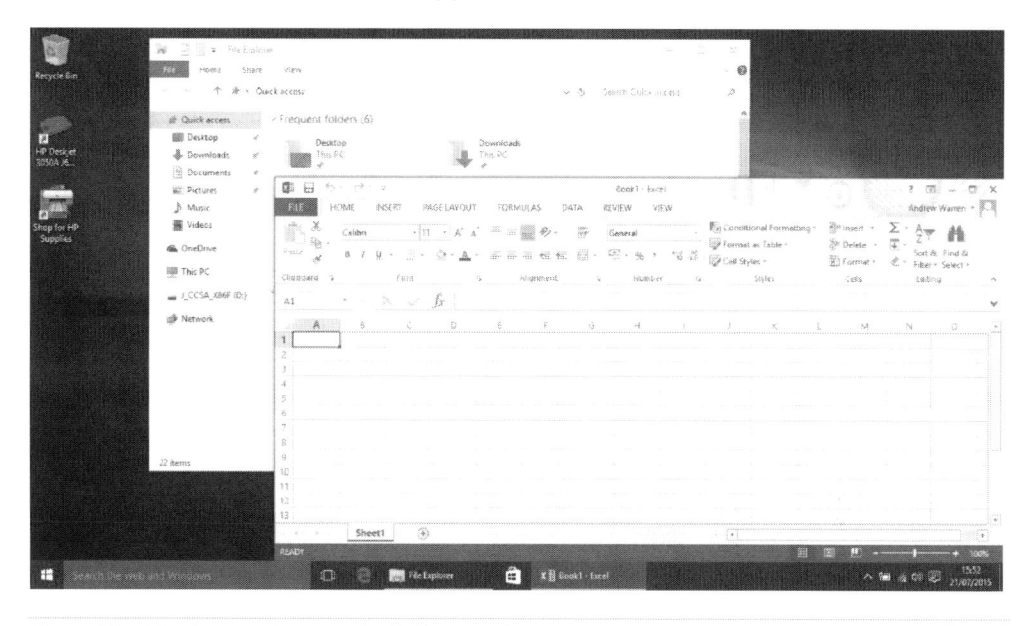

Figure 83.– Viewing running apps in desktop mode

Chapter 5 - Working with Apps

This page left intentionally blank

Chapter 6

Security

What you will do in this chapter:

- Configure Windows Firewall
- Use Windows Defender
- Learn about BitLocker drive encryption

Configuring Windows Firewall

What is a firewall?

A firewall is a technology designed to restrict access to a local network or local host (a device on a network). Its purpose is to help to ensure that only permitted network communications[21] can occur within the protected network.

Note: Since some malicious software relies on network communications to get installed on network devices (hosts), it is important to control network traffic.

Some firewall technologies are based on dedicated hardware devices. These hardware devices are usually placed at the physical boundaries to the protected network and create a perimeter network through which all inbound and outbound traffic must travel. These firewalls are configured with rules that allow for the control of this network traffic.

Windows 10 includes a software only firewall. This software program is designed to filter inbound and outbound traffic according to predefined but configurable rules that allow or block network traffic into and out of the local host.

Windows Firewall

You would not normally be required to reconfigure the Windows Firewall; you can usually rely upon the settings of your wireless home hub and the default Windows Firewall rules to protect you. However, occasionally, you might need to adjust the rules to support a new app's requirements. For example, some online games require particular network communications to function correctly.

Note: Where this is the case, after installing your game (or other app) check the app's documentation for information about the firewall changes you must make.

---

[21] *Also known as network traffic.*

Chapter 6 - Security

To configure Windows Firewall:

1. Open **Settings**.
2. Touch **Network & Internet**.
3. Touch **WiFi** and then touch **Windows Firewall**.

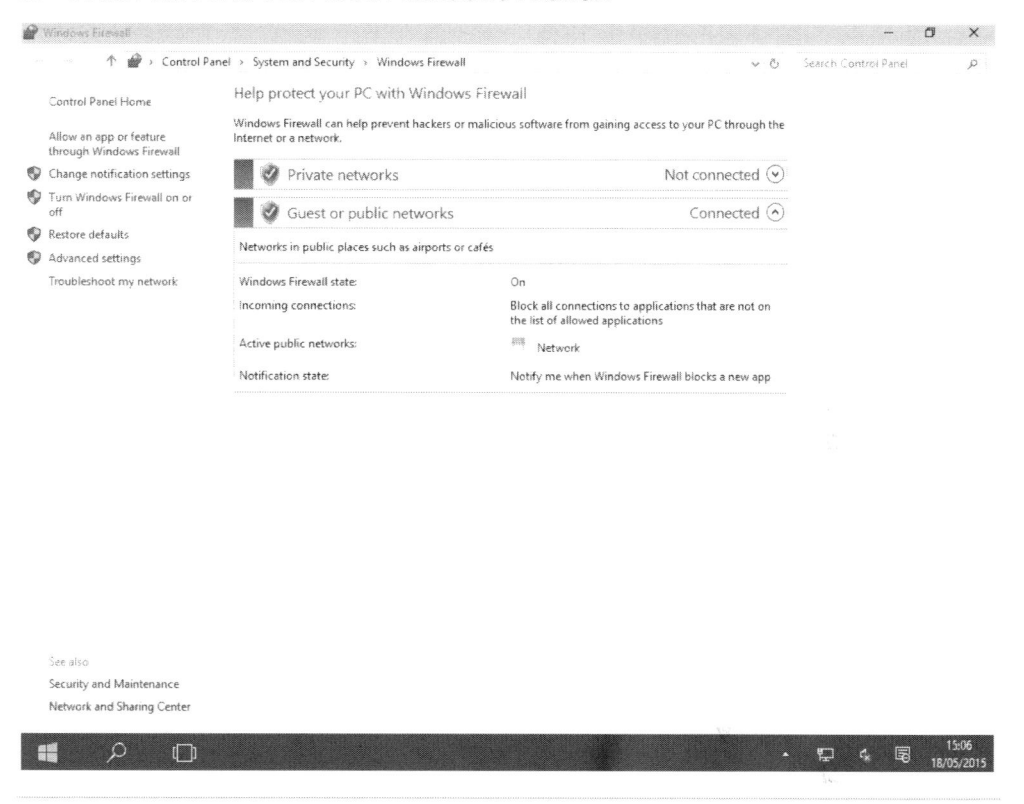

Figure 84.– Windows Firewall settings

You can then configure the following options:

- **Allow an app or feature through Windows Firewall**. This enables you to let a network app communicate through the firewall (see below).

- **Change notification settings**. Enables you to block notifications from Windows Firewall. These notifications might relate to blocked network traffic, and so generally should not be changed.

- **Turn Windows Firewall on or off**. You should not normally disable the Windows Firewall; doing so leaves your computer at risk from malicious software.

Note: If you are troubleshooting an app or feature, and suspect that it doesn't work because of Windows Firewall, disabling the firewall, albeit temporarily, can help identify that issue.

- **Advanced settings**. If you know what you're doing, you can use the advanced firewall settings to create your own custom firewall and connection security rules[22].

In addition to the preceding options, you can also see to what type of network your device is connected. Windows identifies each network that you connect to and asks you to define it as being a public network (the default) or a private network. It is possible to apply different firewall settings based on the network profile you selected. More restrictive firewall rules apply for public networks than for private networks, such as your home network or your workplace network[23].

Allowing apps through the firewall

For most situations, allowing an app through your firewall is likely to be the only configuration you will need to undertake for Windows Firewall. To allow an app through the firewall, use the following procedure:

1. From Windows Firewall, touch **Allow an app or feature through Windows Firewall**.
2. In the **Allow apps to communicate through Windows Firewall** window, touch **Change settings**.

---

[22] *A connection security rule is an advanced feature of Windows that enables you to secure network traffic in transit by using advanced authentication options and encryption technologies to help to protect your information.*

[23] *To reconfigure your network profile, use the Network and Sharing Center link on the Windows Firewall page.*

Chapter 6 - Security

3. Select (for both public and private networks) the appropriate check boxes for the apps and features you want to allow through Windows Firewall and then touch **OK**.

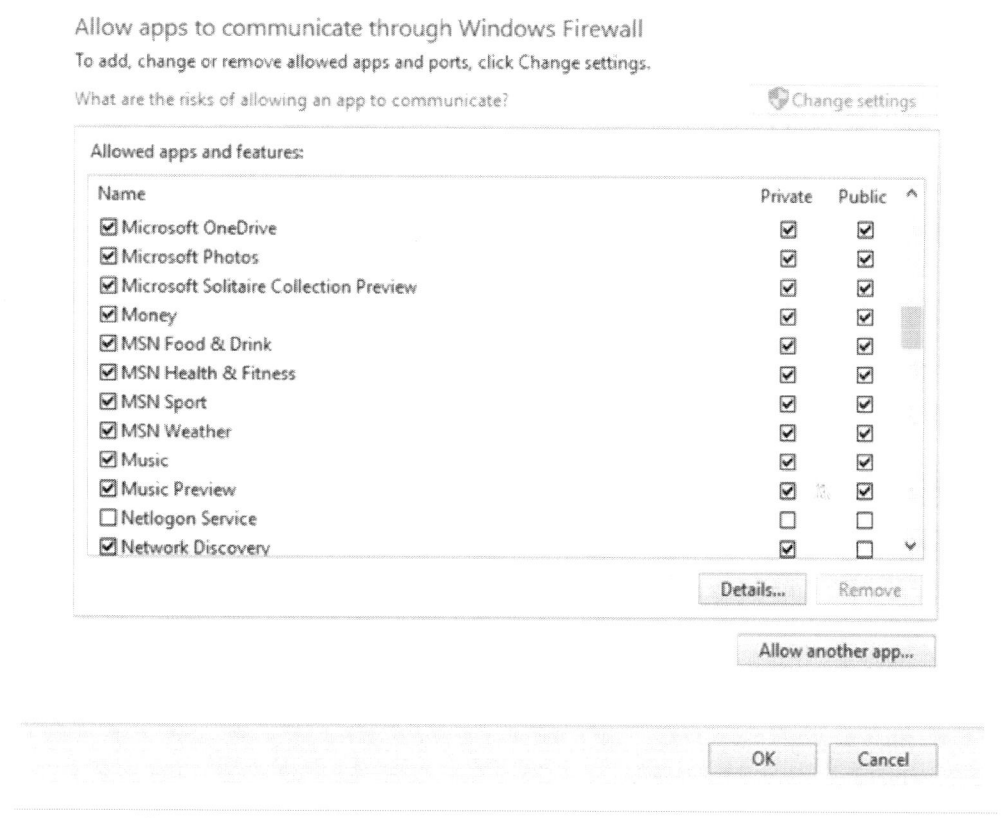

Figure 85.— Allowing an app through Windows Firewall

4. If the app you want is not listed touch **Allow another app**.

5. In the **Allow an app** window, browse and locate the app you want to allow through the firewall. Windows opens a window that enables you to select executable (.EXE) files. You must know where your app installed in order to configure this behaviour.

Note: You can only configure desktop apps here. Windows Store apps do not require this level of manual configuration.

6. Select the **Network Types**, touch **OK**, and then touch **Add**.

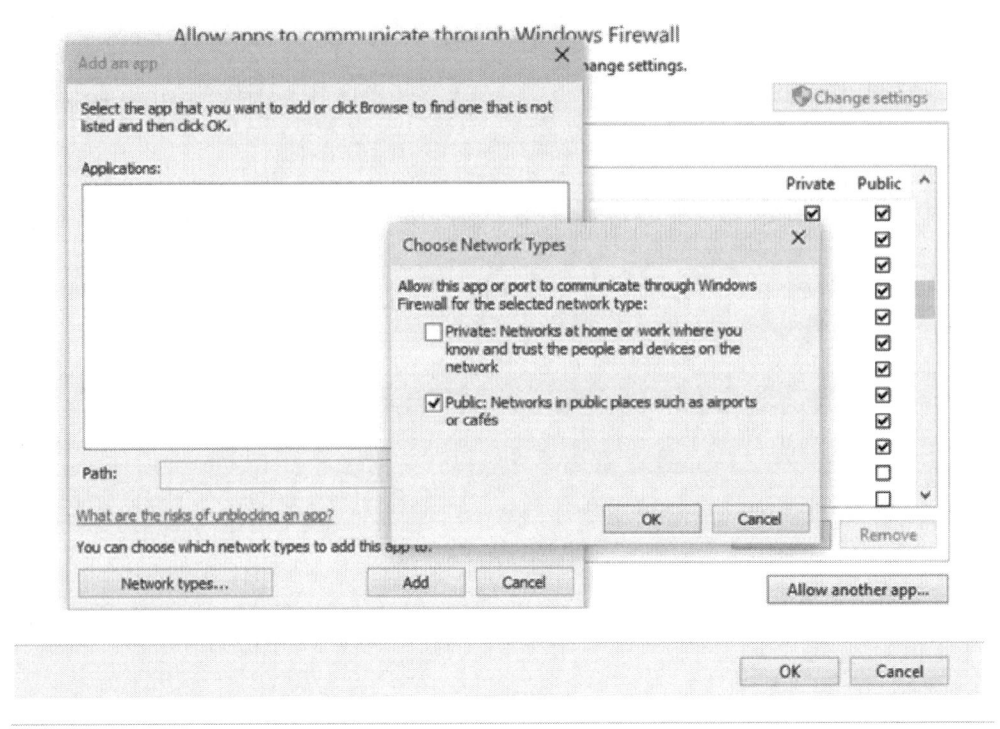

Figure 86.– Allowing additional apps through the firewall

7. In the **Allow apps to communicate through Windows Firewall** window, touch **OK**.

If, at a subsequent time, you want to revert this change, you can either manually clear the check boxes that allow an app through the firewall, or you can just touch **Restore defaults** in the **Windows Firewall** window.

Using Windows Defender

What is malicious software?

Malicious software is any program designed to disrupt normal behaviour of your device. The purpose of this disruption may be to launch adverts on your device, to cause mischief, or it may be more serious and be an attempt to gather information from your device for criminal purposes.

Consequently, it is important to take steps to help to ensure that your device is protected from malicious software. We have already seen that User Account Control can help by warning you when a software configuration change is launched. The last section described how Windows Firewall can help to block undesirable network traffic in an effort to guard against malicious software.

Windows Defender

Another tool in your arsenal against malicious software is Windows Defender. This app provides both anti-malware and antivirus protection for your device. By default, Windows Defender is running all of the time providing real-time protection. Generally, there is little for you to do; suspect programs are isolated automatically, and Windows Update keeps the antivirus and anti-malware up to date to guard against new and emerging malicious software threats.

Chapter 6 - Security

However, if you want to view or configure Windows Defender settings:

1. Open **Settings**.
2. Touch **Update & security**.
3. Touch **Windows Defender**.

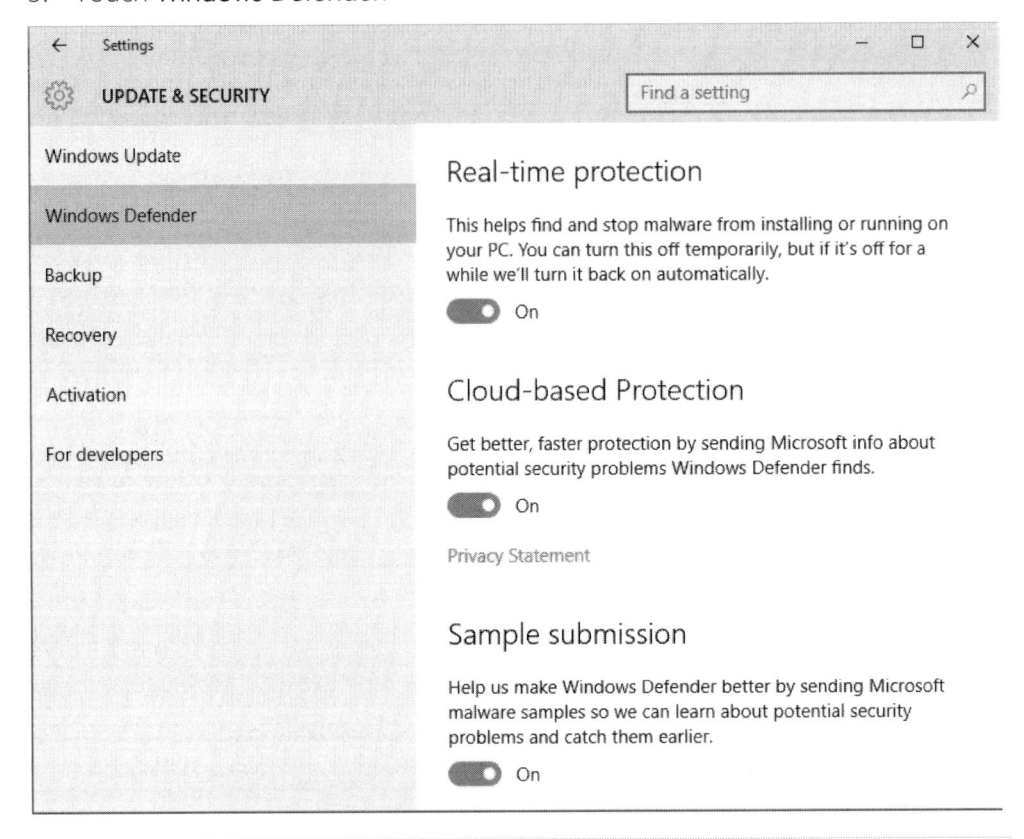

Figure 87.– Configuring Windows Defender

4. You can then enable or disable real-time protection, cloud protection, and define exclusions. Exclusions are those executables that Windows Defender might class as suspicious but that you know to be safe.

5. You can also launch the Windows Defender app from here by touching **Use Windows Defender**.

Running a scan

As scans occur automatically, you won't normally need to run one manually. But you can do so from the Windows Defender app. On the **Home** tab, touch **Scan now** to perform a quick scan. If you want to perform a more through scan, touch **Full** and then touch **Scan now**.

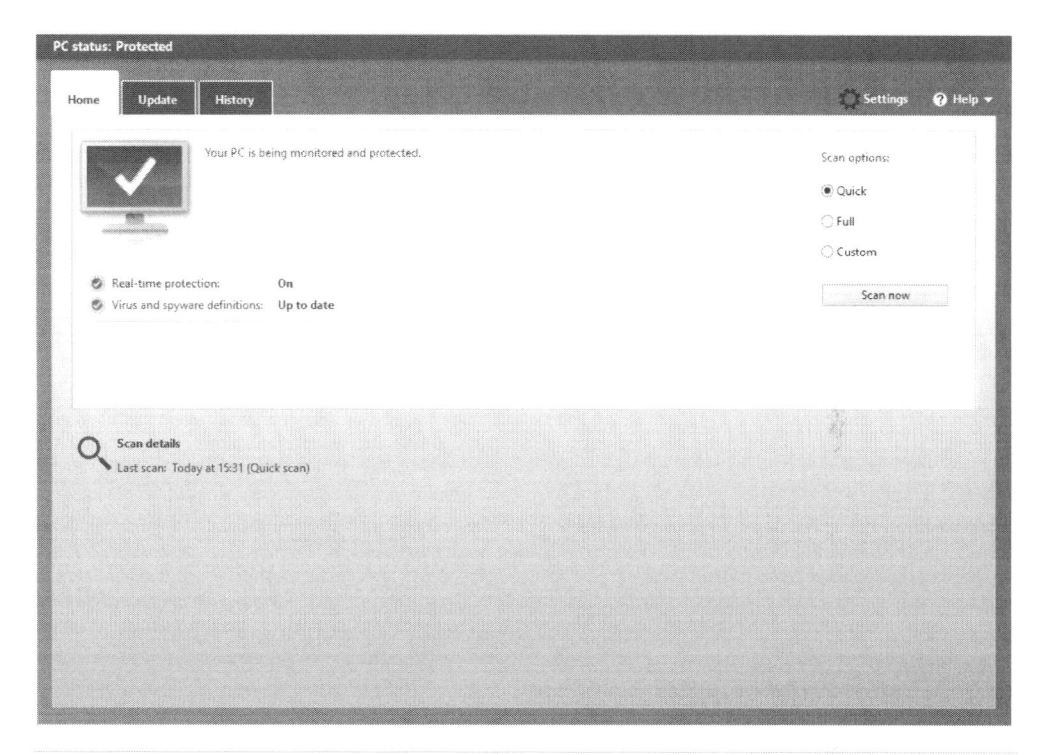

Figure 88.– Running Windows Defender

Chapter 6 - Security

Scan history

From within the app, on the **History** tab, you can view quarantined items, allowed items, and all detected items. Select the appropriate option and then touch **View details**.

If any suspicious software has been identified and quarantined, you can then remove it from your computer, or, if you think the software is not malicious, restore it to its original location.

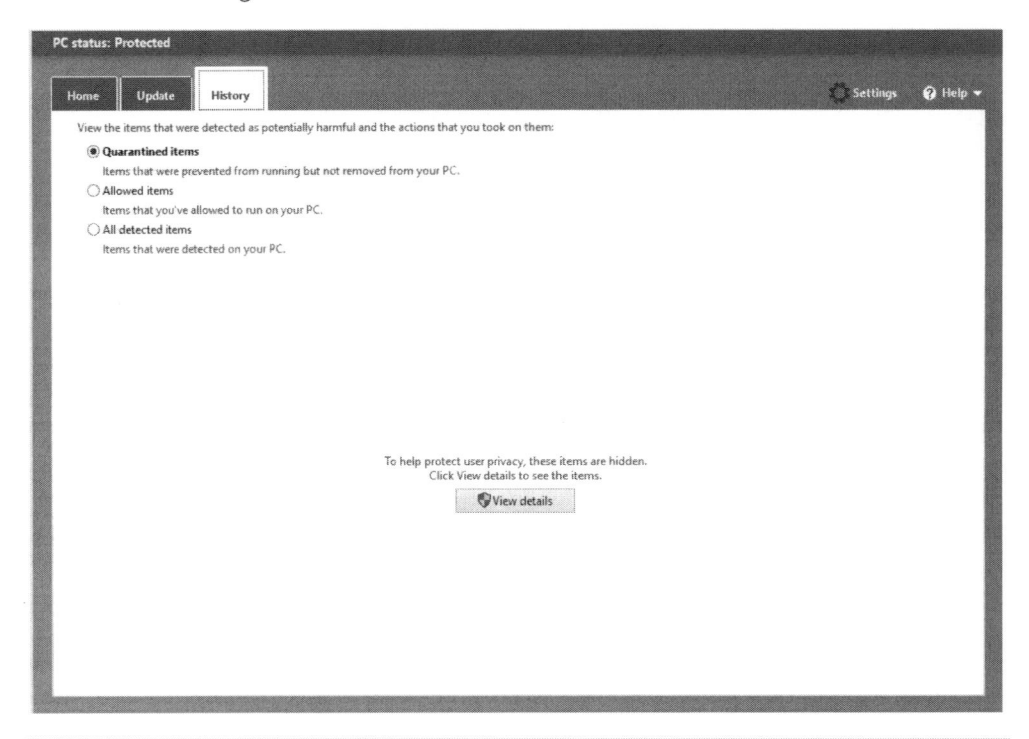

Figure 89.— Scan history in Windows Defender

Chapter 6 - Security

Keeping Windows Defender up to date

It is vital to keep Windows Defender up to date. Windows Update, the service that keeps Windows 10 up to date, also updates Windows Defender patterns. You can check whether you have recently installed updates for Windows Defender via the **Update** tab in the Windows Defender app.

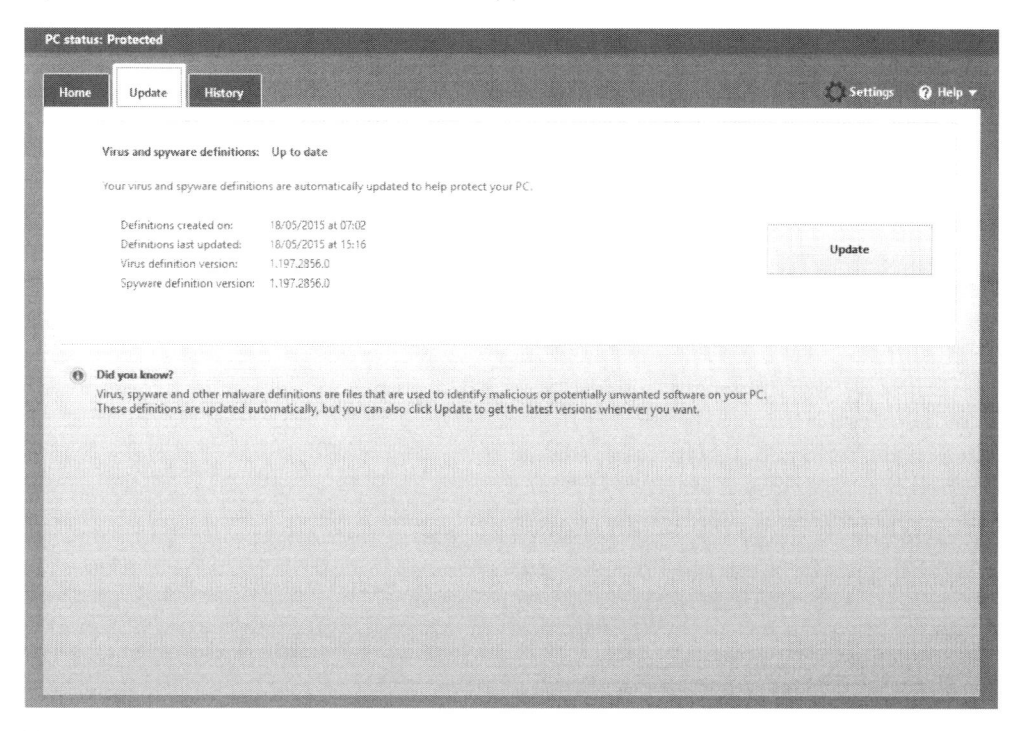

Figure 90.– Checking for Windows Defender updates

Implementing BitLocker

The importance of drive encryption

These days, we use our phones and tablets to store contact information, and to access sensitive data, like our bank accounts online. Whilst it is important to protect your device against malicious software by using Windows Defender and Windows Firewall, losing your device (or having it stolen) represents a significant risk to your personal data.

Although Windows cannot prevent your device from being left on a train or stolen from your rucksack, it can help protect the data stored on the device should either of the preceding things occur[24].

Aside from the whole device going astray, with the proliferation of memory sticks and storage cards being used to hold our data, it's getting all too easy to mislay sensitive information.

Using drive encryption provides an easy way to help to mitigate these risks. Microsoft introduced Windows BitLocker with Windows Vista. BitLocker enables you to encrypt the hard drives (both internal and removal) of your device. To access the device's storage, you must decrypt the drive, usually by entering a PIN or password, or using a digital key stored in a smartcard.

---

[24] *Many organizations can apply policies to users' devices that allow administrators to wipe content from devices which have been lost or stolen. This is not usually possible with personal devices that are not managed by corporate device policies.*

Enabling BitLocker

BitLocker is not enabled by default. To enable BitLocker:

1. Open **File Explorer**.

2. Touch and hold the drive you want to secure with BitLocker. From the context menu, touch **Turn BitLocker on**.

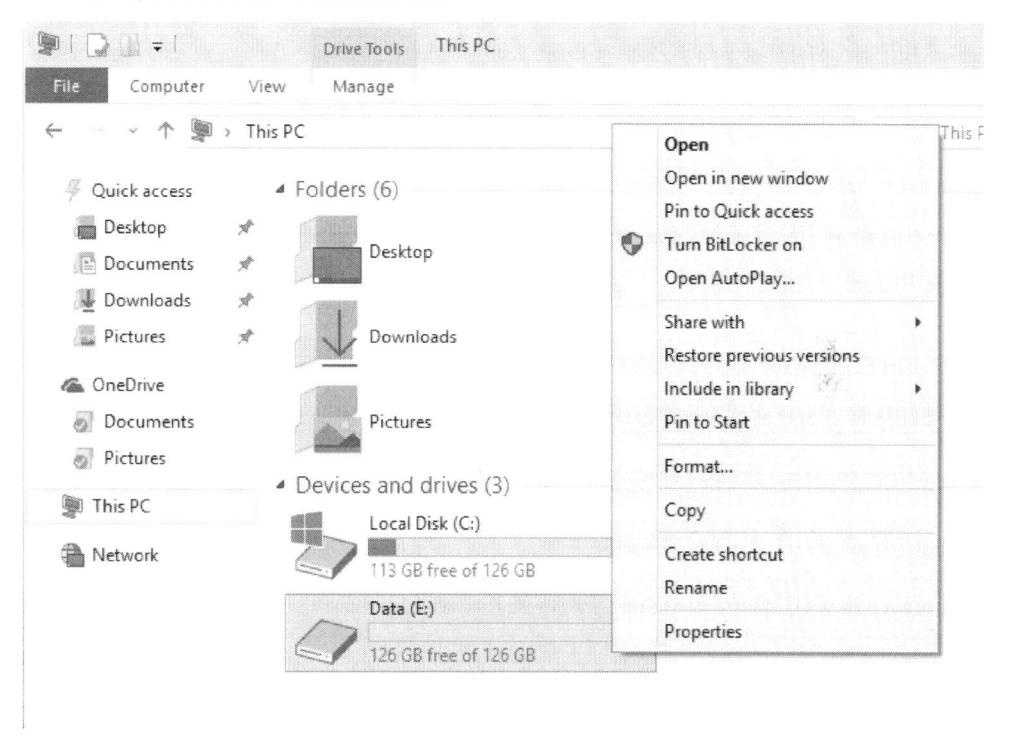

Figure 91.– Enabling BitLocker

3. Windows checks that your device supports the requirements of BitLocker and then scans the drive[25]. You can then choose how to unlock the drive.

---

[25] For the system drive (usually drive C), BitLocker requires a Trusted Platform Module (TPM) to handle the keys used for drive encryption. If your device does not have a TPM installed (and most tablets and laptops do), then you must make some additional configuration changes to encrypt the internal system drive. A TPM is not required for other drives.

Chapter 6 - Security

4. You can choose either **Use a password to unlock the drive** or **Use my smart card to unlock the drive**[26]. Choosing a password is more usual. Enter your password and touch **Next**.

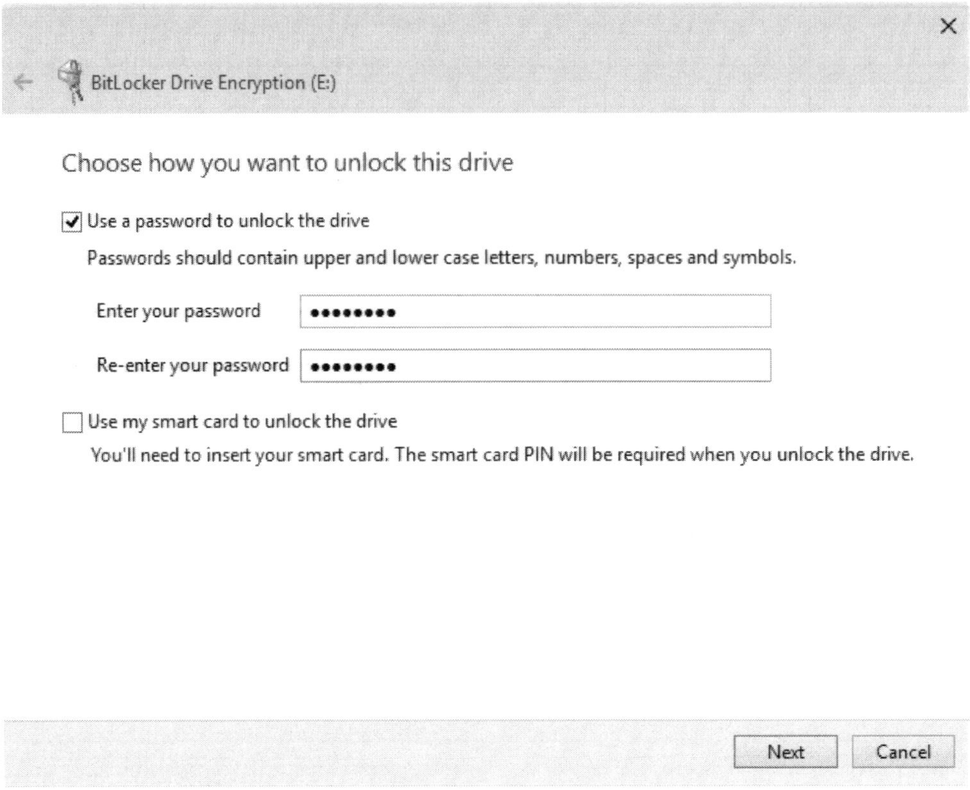

Figure 92.– Configuring BitLocker

---

[26] *A smart card is a device much like a credit card with memory and a small processor installed that is used by many organizations for authenticating users.*

Chapter 6 - Security

5. You are then prompted to save the recovery key. This is used in the event that you forget your password. Select **Save to your Microsoft account** and touch **Next**. If you prefer to save elsewhere, select your preferred method.

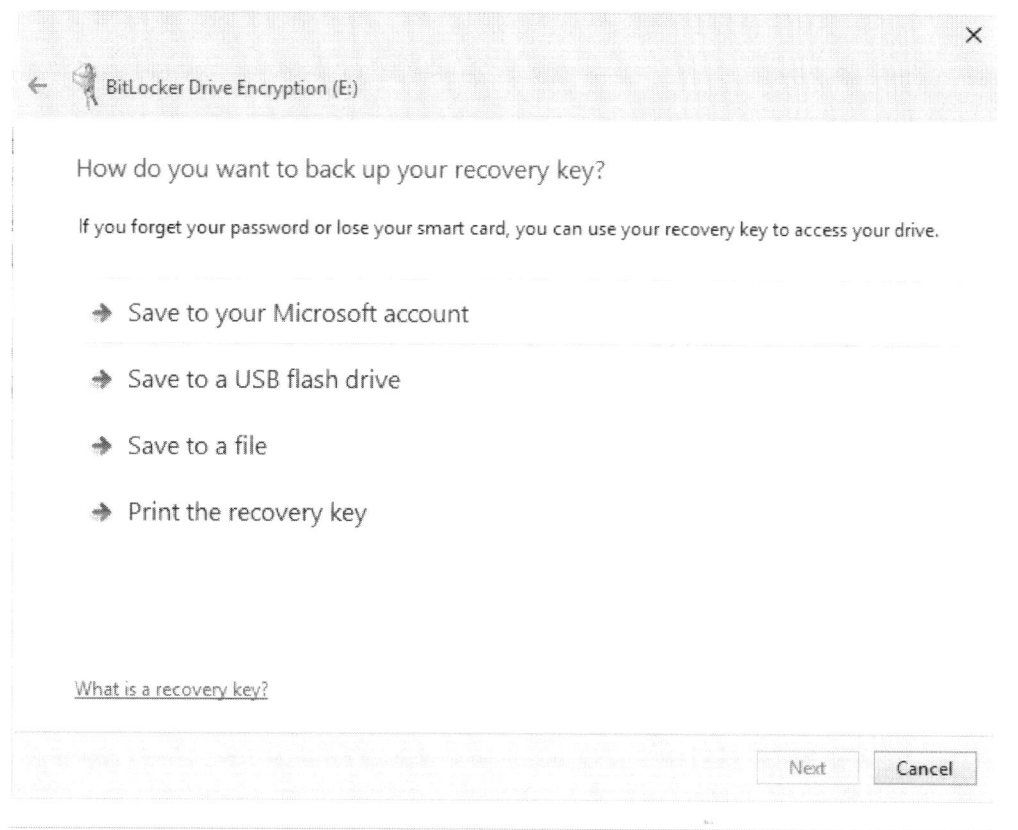

Figure 93.– Saving the recovery key

6. Finally, on the **Are you ready to encrypt this drive?** page, when ready, touch **Start encrypting**.

Using BitLocker drives

There are no special considerations for using BitLocker encrypted drives. When you insert a protected drive, you are prompted for your password or smartcard as appropriate. If you forget your password, then you can use your recovery key to access the drive and set a new password.

Windows also makes things easy for drives that you often use on a specific device. For example, if you use a particular USB memory stick on your device often, when you unlock the drive, you can set an option to remember the unlock password on that device. This saves you from having to enter the password each time you mount the drive.

> **Note**: Enabling this feature does compromise security a little. After all, if both the memory stick and device are lost or stolen together, the device can be unlocked without the password.

Encrypting the operating system drive

If your device has only a single drive in which to store the operating system and data, then you should consider encrypting the system drive. This provides the greatest protection since the entire device can be protected – not just the removable data drives.

However, encrypting the system drive usually requires a Trusted Platform Module (TPM). Most devices have this capability these days, and it can be enabled or disabled from your device's BIOS settings[27]. The TPM stores the encryption keys and related data so that you do not need to use external memory sticks to store them. You can combine the use of a TPM with a PIN or password for additional security.

> **Note**: You cannot move your device's hard drive to another device when encrypted with BitLocker using a TPM: for example, if your device failed and was replaced and it's hard drive moved to the new device. You must first turn off BitLocker on the installed drive. This limitation does not apply to drives encrypted without a TPM, such as removable drives.

---

[27] *To access your device's BIOS, refer to your hardware vendor's product documentation. For my Lenovo tablet, I must start the device by holding the power button AND the volume up button until the special startup menu is displayed. I can then use the touch screen to start the BIOS.*

Manage BitLocker

To manage BitLocker settings, from **Control Panel**, **System and Security**, touch **BitLocker Drive Encryption**.

Note: As a shortcut, touch and hold a BitLocker encrypted drive and touch **Manage BitLocker**.

From the **BitLocker Drive Encryption** window, you can:

- **Back up your recovery key**. Enables you to back up your recovery key to an alternate location.

- **Change password**. Enables you to change your BitLocker password.

- **Remove password**. Enables you to remove your BitLocker password.

- **Add smart card**. Enables you to configure a new or different smartcard for drive unlock.

- **Turn on auto-unlock**. Enables you to automatically unlock a drive when used.

- **Turn off BitLocker**. Enables you to turn off BitLocker for the selected drive.

BitLocker Drive Encryption
Help protect your files and folders from unauthorised access by protecting your drives with BitLocker.

Operating system drive

C: BitLocker off

Fixed data drives

Data (E:) BitLocker on

- Back up your recovery key
- Change password
- Remove password
- Add smart card
- Turn on auto-unlock
- Turn off BitLocker

Removable data drives - BitLocker To Go
Insert a removable USB flash drive to use BitLocker To Go.

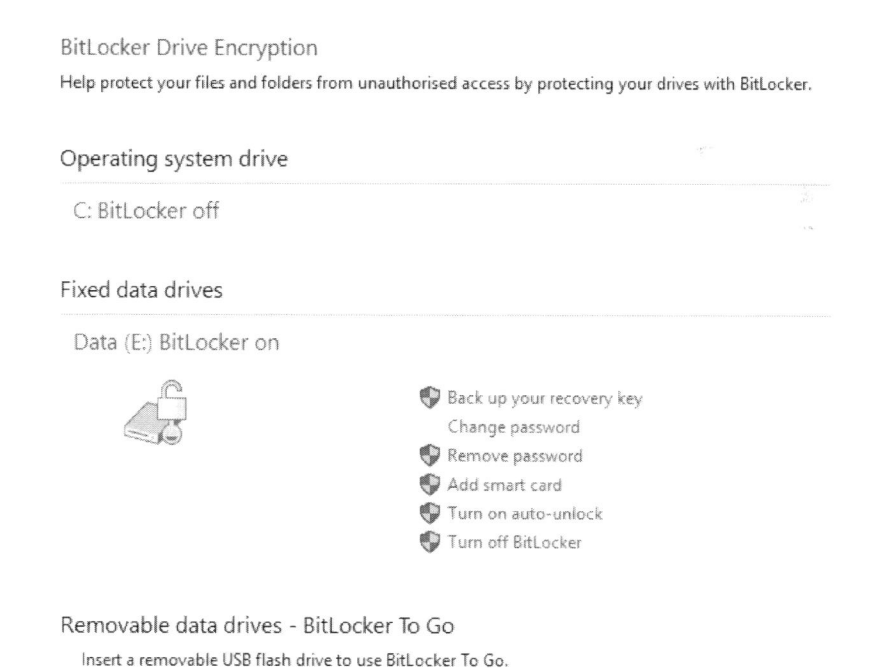

Figure 94.– Managing BitLocker settings

Chapter 6 - Security

The available options depend upon what type of drive has been selected in the window: operating system drive, fixed data drives, removable data drives (referred to as BitLocker to Go).

Chapter 7

Connecting Peripherals

What you will do in this chapter:

- Connect a printer
- Configure Bluetooth devices
- Manage storage devices

Chapter 7 - Connecting Peripherals

Connecting Printers

Initial setup

Connecting and configuring a printer is not very complicated. Generally, the process is as follows:

1. Obtain the printer driver[28] and install on your device. Usually, the printer will come with a driver DVD which you can use to install the driver. The driver setup program is a desktop app and you should use the procedure mentioned previously in this book for running the setup program.

Note: If your device does not have a DVD drive as is likely the case with a tablet, then you must download the driver from the printer vendor's website and run it that way. Open your web browser and navigate to your search page. Enter the printer make and model number and the word driver in the search box. Ensure that any driver you download is from the vendor's website. Also, make sure you obtain a 32-bit or 64-bit driver as required.

2. Connect your printer to your device. Usually, this will be via a USB connection. If your device does not have a USB connection, you must connect to the printer using Wi-Fi.

Note: Configuring the Wi-Fi settings on a printer usually requires connecting it to a device via USB the first time, so this may prove a challenge!

3. Turn on the printer. Your Windows device should recognise the printer and set it up using the printer driver you previously installed.

4. Your printer is now ready for use.

---

[28] *A printer driver is a software interface that sits between Windows and the physical printer. It understands how to interpret general Windows instructions to manage paper size, resolution, and fonts and can translate those into specific hardware instructions for the printer.*

Installing an HP LaserJet P1102W

By way of example, the following procedure is used to install a HP LaserJet P1102W.

1. Search for the driver software on Google using a specific search term. It is important that you mention the make and model of the printer. If the printer you have predates Windows 10 (as is the case below), you can usually use a driver from an earlier version of Windows.

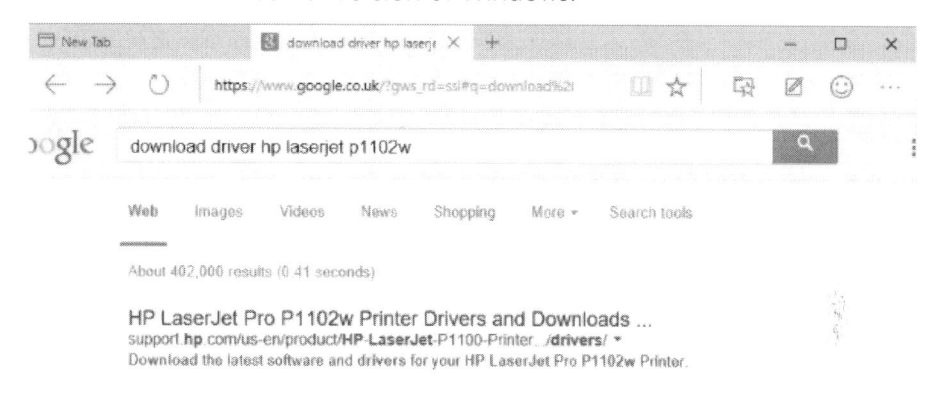

Figure 95.– Searching for the printer driver

2. Ensure that the website is the hardware vendor's – in this case, Hewlett Packard.

3. Download the driver software from HP.

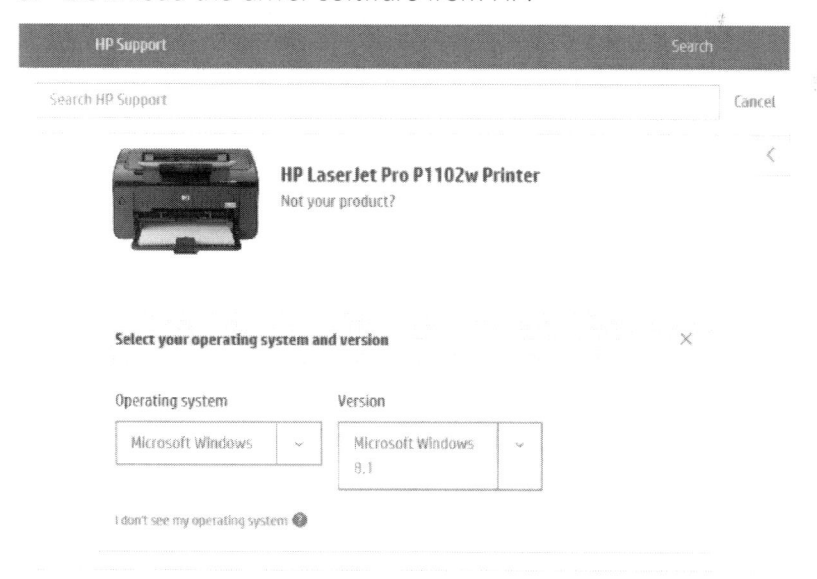

Figure 96.– Selecting and downloading the appropriate driver

Chapter 7 - Connecting Peripherals

4. Install the driver. Once the download is complete, you can launch the installation routine by touching **Run** at the bottom of the Edge browser window. You may be prompted by **User Account Control** to confirm that you wish to install the driver and related software.

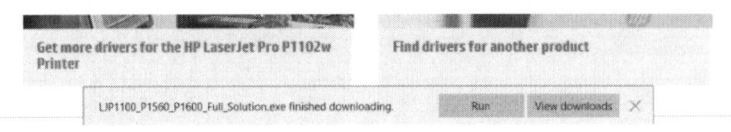

Figure 97.– Launching the installation program to install the driver

5. Configure the driver and related printer software. In this instance, a graphical wizard launches and prompts the installer through the process of configuring the software. Touch **USB install** and then touch **Begin Setup**. In the **Animated Getting Started guide**, touch **Install Printer Software**.

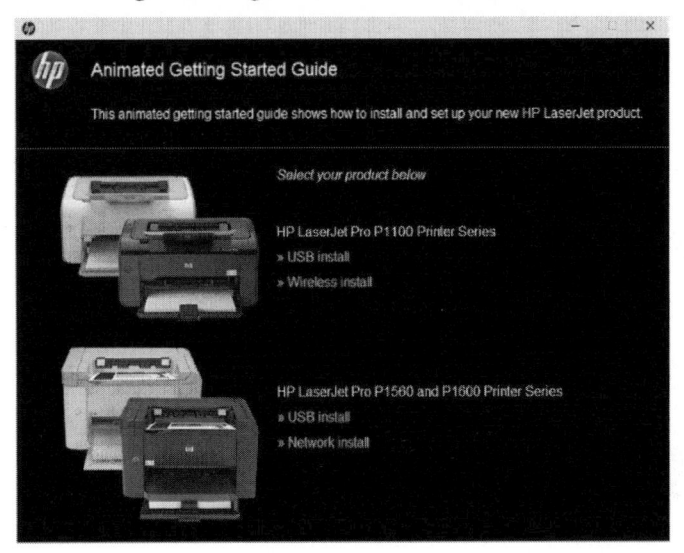

Figure 98.– Select the type of connection

6. You may be prompted by **User Account Control** to continue. Touch **Yes**.

Chapter 7 - Connecting Peripherals

7. In the **HP LaserJet Professional P1100-P1560-P1600 Series** window, touch **Next**.

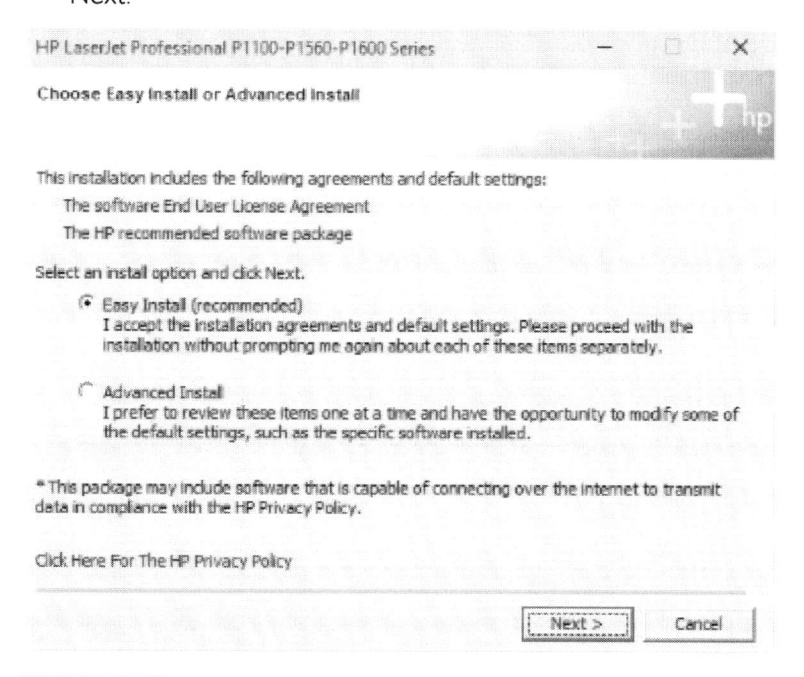

Figure 99.– Choose the installation method

8. In the **Printers** list, touch **HP LaserJet Professional P1100w** and touch **Next**.

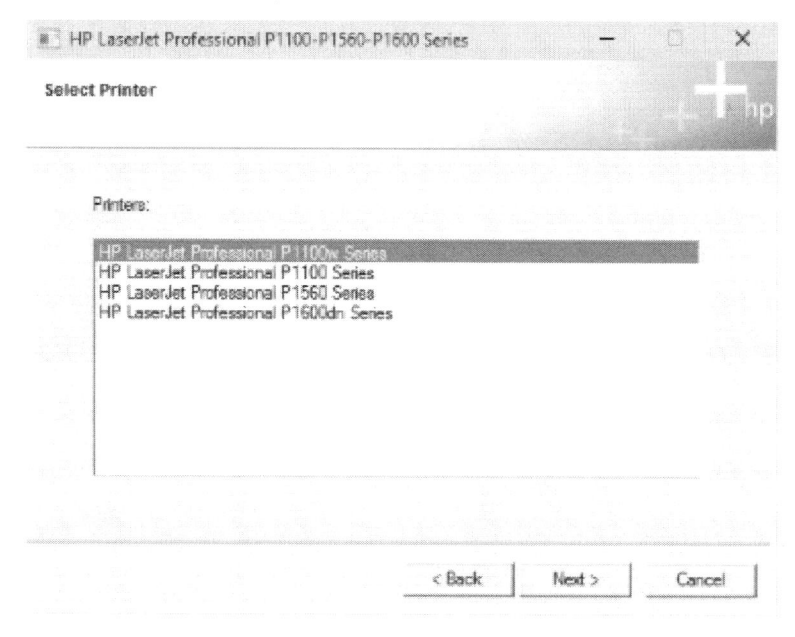

Figure 100.– Select the printer model

Chapter 7 - Connecting Peripherals

9. In the Printer Connections window, touch **Configure to print using USB** and touch **Next**. Your driver software is installed.

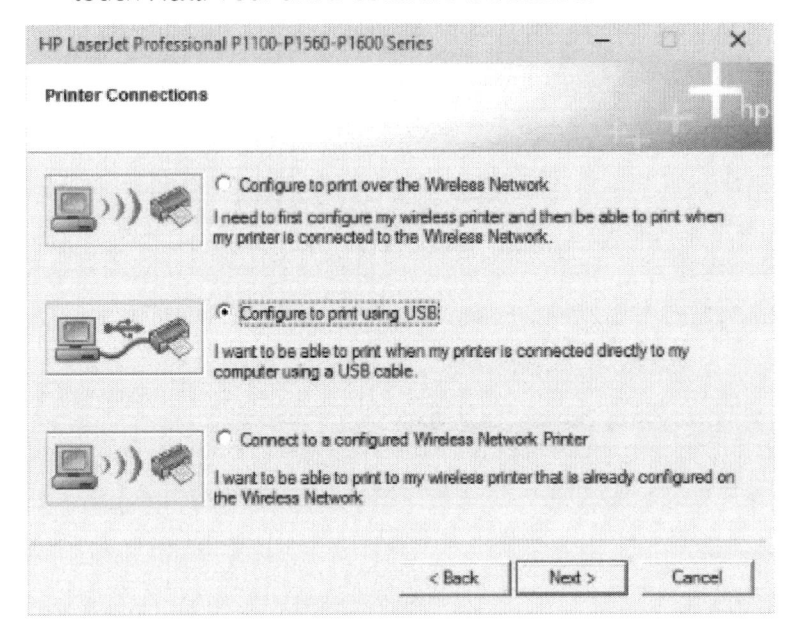

Figure 101.– Select the connection method

10. When the **Configure to print using USB** window displays, power up your printer and connect it. Windows recognizes the device and initializes the drivers.

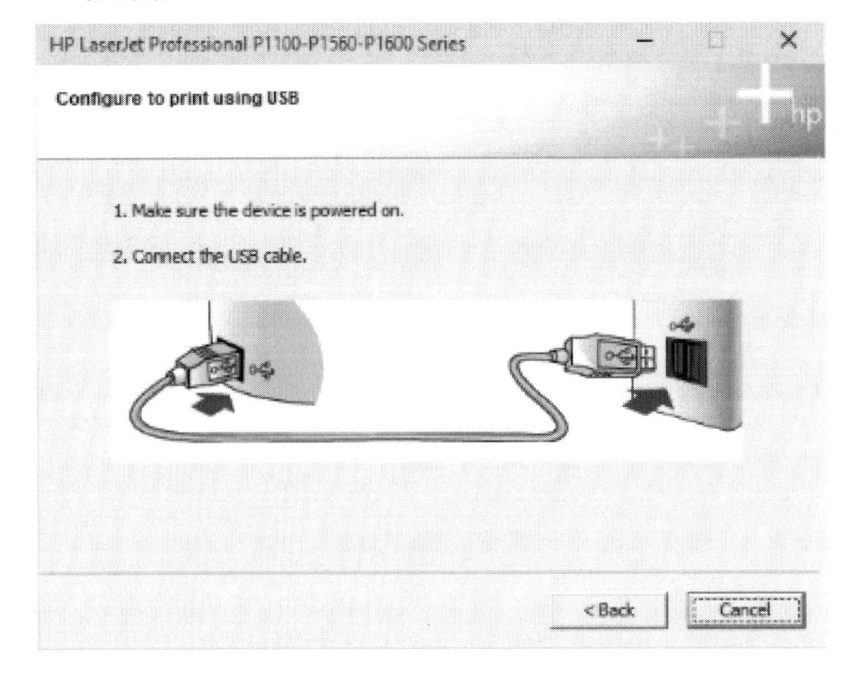

Figure 102.– Connecting the printer

Chapter 7 - Connecting Peripherals

11. In the **Congratulations** page, clear the **Register your product** check box and then touch **Next**. A test page should print. Touch **Finish** to complete the installation.

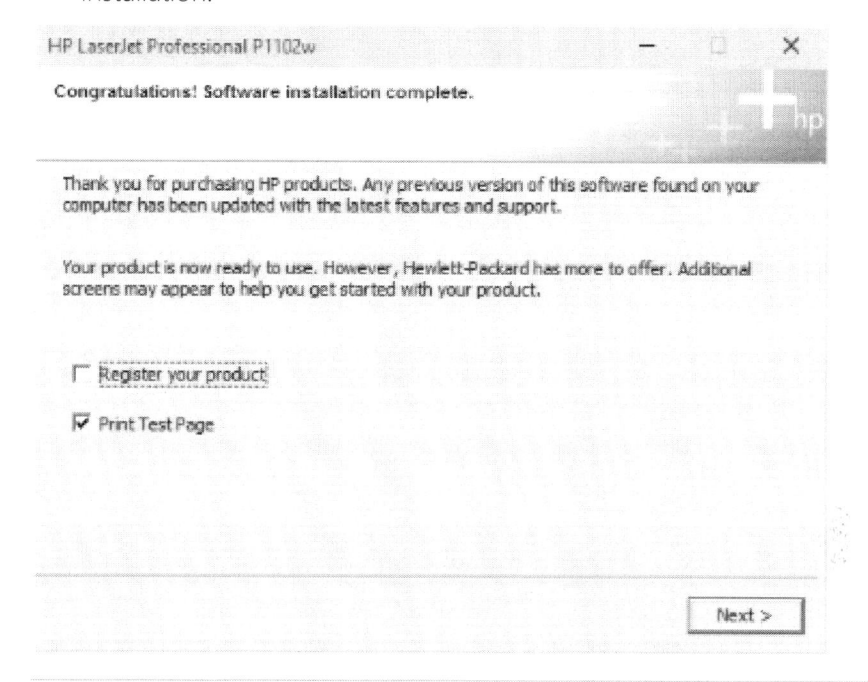

Figure 103.– Completing the installation

Chapter 7 - Connecting Peripherals

Managing a Printer

Once your printer is installed, you can configure its properties. To do this, use the following procedure:

1. Open **Settings** and then touch **Devices**.
2. Touch **Printers & scanners**.
3. In the details pane, touch **Devices and printers**.

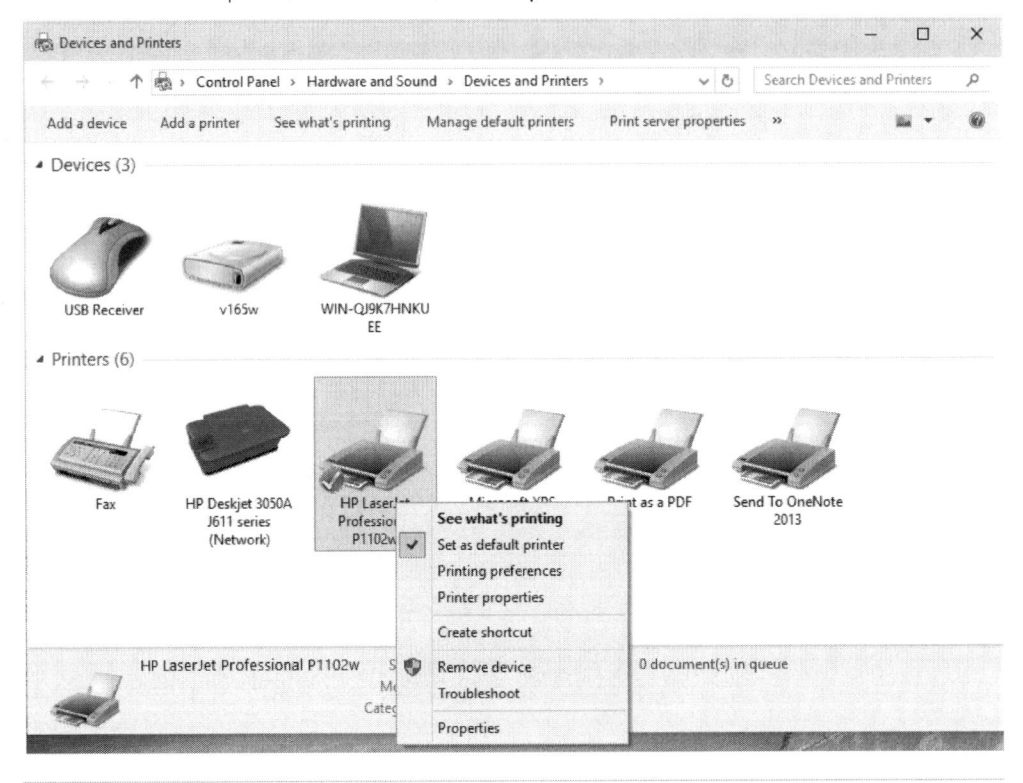

Figure 104.– Devices and printers

Chapter 7 - Connecting Peripherals

4. In the **Devices and Printers** window, touch and hold your printer. Touch **Printer Preferences**.

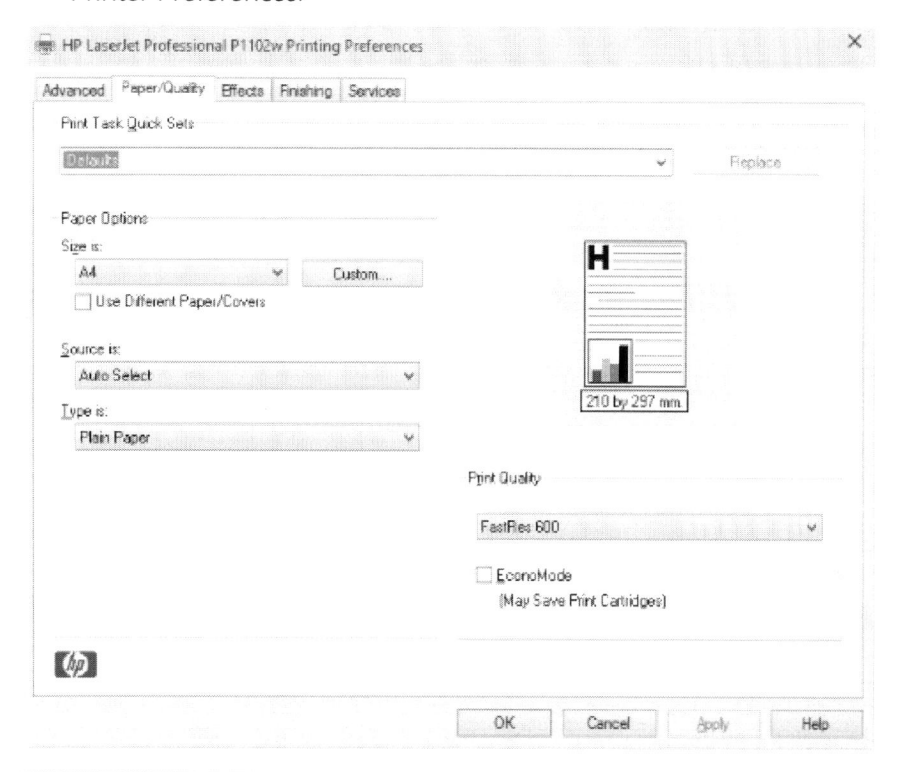

Figure 105.– Printing preferences

5. In the **Printing Preferences** window, configure the settings of your printer. You can configure the following properties and options:

- **Paper/Quality**. Specify the physical paper size. Define the appropriate paper tray (where applicable). Define the paper type (e.g. plain paper). Configure the resolution for printing.

- **Effects**. Enables you to configure scaling and watermark options.

- **Finishing**. Enables you to define pages per sheet, and options such as printing on both sides of the paper.

Note: These options can also be configured from within your app, for example, by using the Printer settings in Microsoft Office Word.

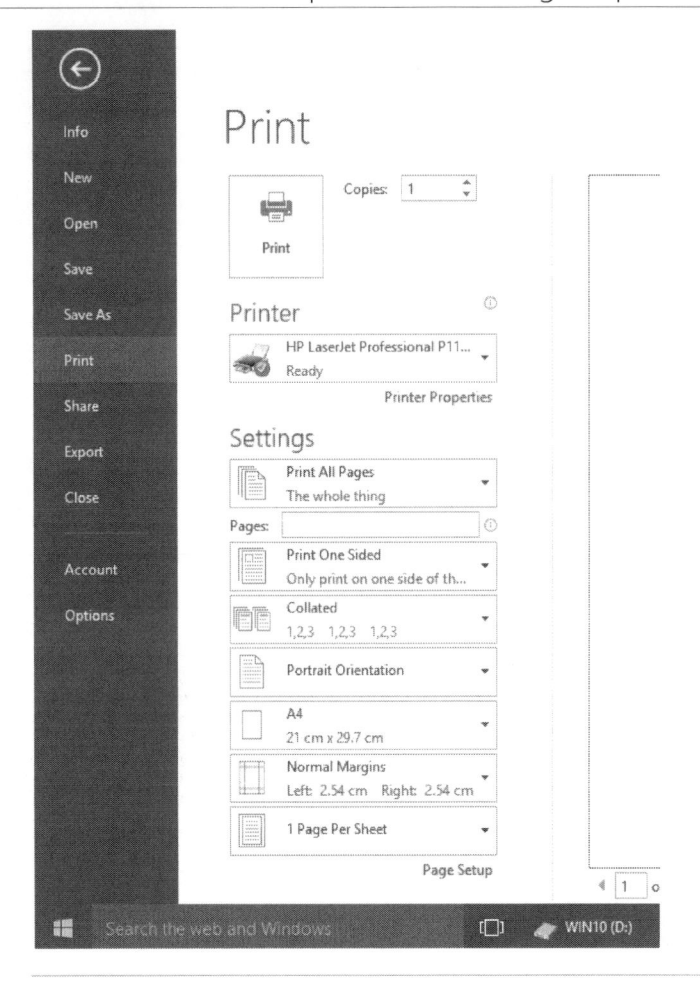

Figure 106.– Configuring printer options from within a desktop app

Chapter 7 - Connecting Peripherals

Configuring Bluetooth

With a device such as a tablet, connecting peripherals using USB is not always possible. Although most devices do provide a Micro USB port, there is generally only one and this is often used for charging the device. Consequently, if you have additional peripherals, such as keyboards and mice, you may wish to connect them by using Bluetooth[29].

Preparing to use Bluetooth

To connect a peripheral to your Windows 10 device using Bluetooth, you will need several things:

- **Ensure that Bluetooth is enabled.** If your tablet is in Flight mode, then all radios are disabled. In addition, some devices have the capability to disable Bluetooth (and Wi-Fi) in the BIOS. Make sure that the Bluetooth radio is enabled. You can do this by opening the Bluetooth icon in the system tray on the taskbar. If it appears in the system tray, then Bluetooth is enabled.

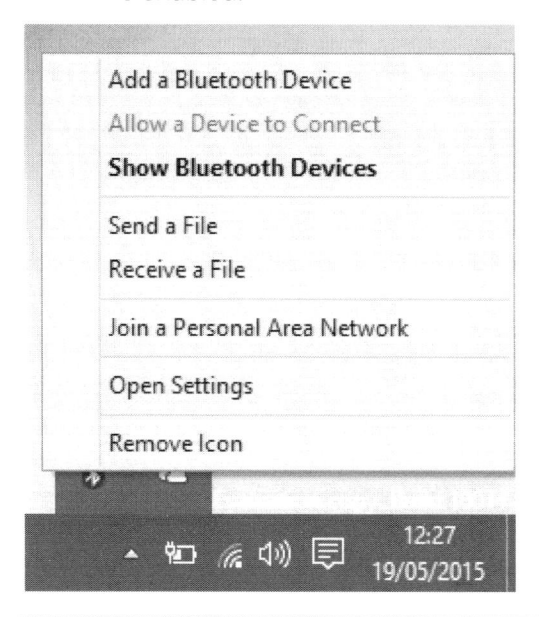

Figure 107.– Verifying that Bluetooth is available

---

[29] *Bluetooth is a short range Wi-Fi protocol used for the connection of peripheral devices including headsets, mice, keyboards, some printers, and media players and mobile phones.*

Chapter 7 - Connecting Peripherals

- **Obtain pairing keys**. When you pair a device[30] such as a phone, to help ensure security, you must enter a key that both devices know. Sometimes, a default key is used (often 0000 to start with), and sometimes, as with a keyboard, Windows generates the key and asks you to enter it on the peripheral device's keypad.

- **Make the peripheral and Windows discoverable**. Bluetooth may be enabled, but unless the device and the peripheral are discoverable, they won't see each other. You can make Windows discoverable using the procedure below, but hardware peripherals vary. Some require a key or button combination to be pressed, resulting (sometimes) in flashing lights to indicate discoverability. In the case of the Microsoft Wedge mouse used below, on the underside is a button that is pressed (and held) to enable discoverability.

---

[30] *Pairing is the term used to describe connecting a device to your Windows device over Bluetooth.*

Chapter 7 - Connecting Peripherals

Connecting a Bluetooth peripheral

To connect a Bluetooth device, use the following procedure:

1. Swipe left from the screen edge and make sure that the Bluetooth tile is active.
2. Touch **All settings** and touch **Devices**.
3. Touch **Bluetooth**. Your device becomes discoverable automatically.

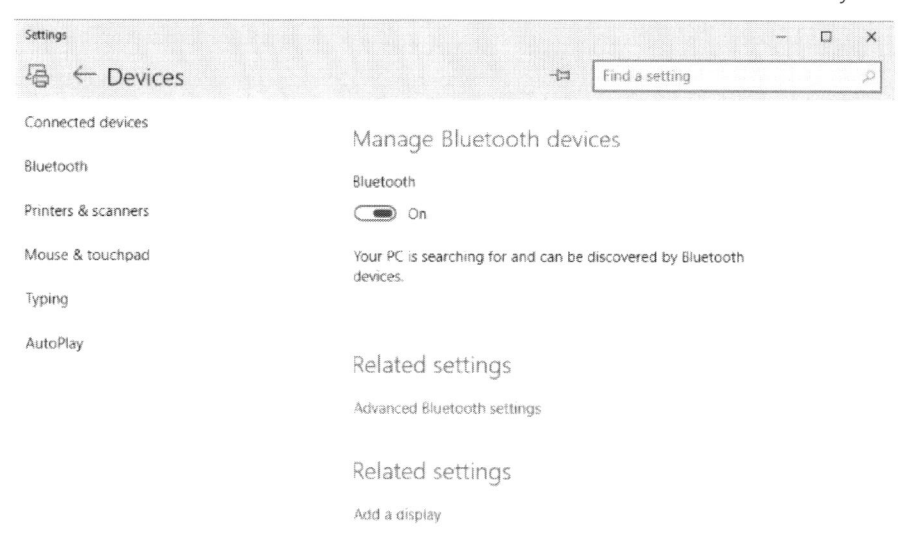

Figure 108.– Enabling discoverability

4. Turn on your peripheral and make it discoverable.

Chapter 7 - Connecting Peripherals

5. Touch the new peripheral device on your Windows screen, in this case, the **Microsoft Wedge Touch Mouse**. Then touch **Pair**.

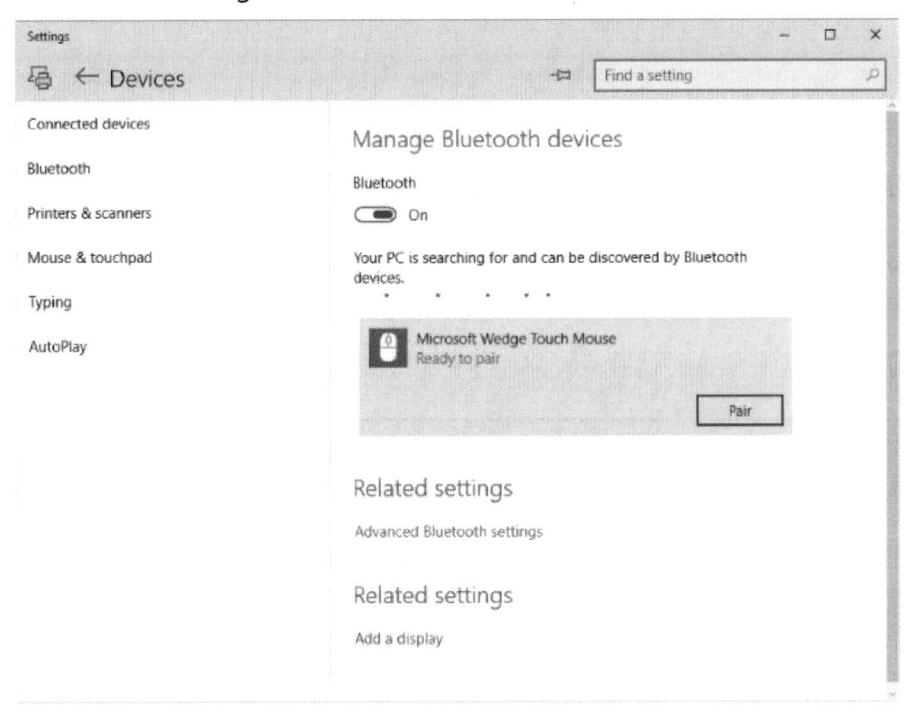

Figure 109.– Ready to pair Bluetooth device

Chapter 7 - Connecting Peripherals

6. Drivers install. Your peripheral is ready (connected).

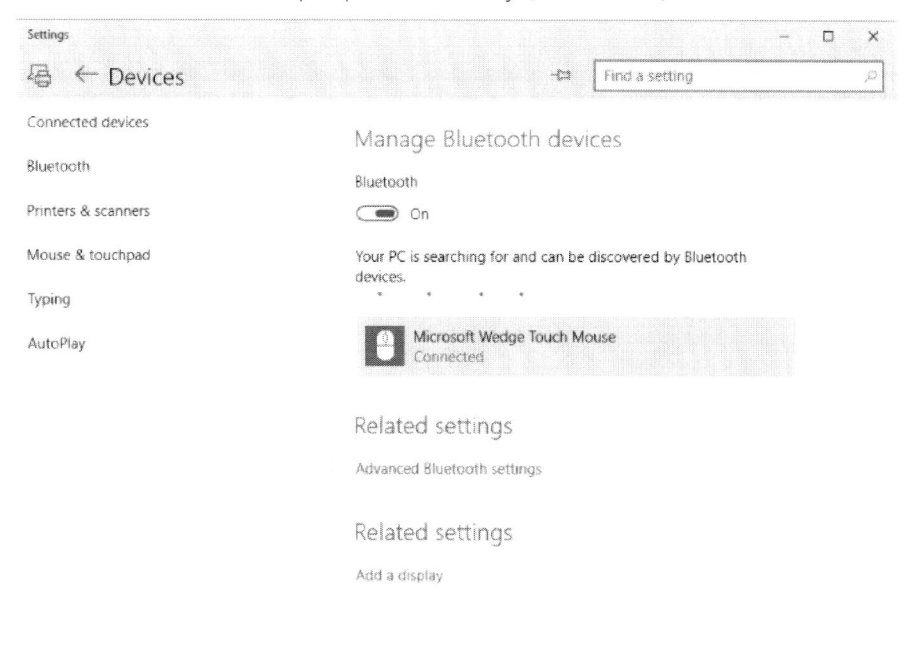

Figure 110.– Bluetooth device is paired and available

Chapter 7 - Connecting Peripherals

You can use the **Advanced Bluetooth Settings** option to:

- Configure notifications about adjacent Bluetooth devices.
- Enable or disable discoverability.
- Determine whether the Bluetooth icon shows in the system tray on the taskbar.

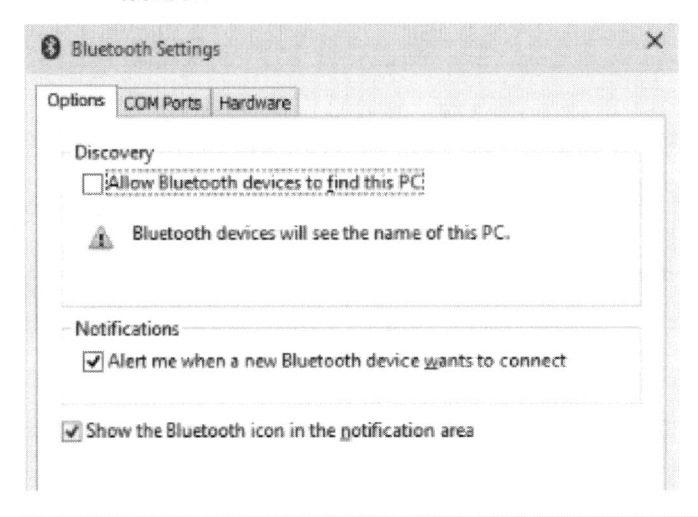

Figure 111.– Advanced Bluetooth settings

Note: the details of this process vary according to the device type and vendor, but are a good guide.

Managing Storage Devices

Windows devices allow you to add additional storage so that you are not constrained by the built-in storage of the device. Consequently, the storage size is not such a big factor when considering the purchase of a Windows 10 device.

My own Lenovo 8 inch Windows tablet has 32 GB of internal storage; this is plenty for the operating system and desktop apps such as Microsoft Office, although I am left with only around 8GB. However, as the device supports Micro SD card expansion and provides a (single) Micro USB port, I can add additional storage as I need. Currently, all my videos and music is installed on a 64 GB Micro SD card.

There is nothing complicated about adding storage to Windows. Simply insert the storage device and Windows installs any required drivers. If the storage device comes unformatted, you may need to create a partition and format it before the storage can be used.

Chapter 7 - Connecting Peripherals

Adding a storage card

You can use the following procedure to format a storage device:

1. Insert the storage device. If it correctly formatted, there is nothing more to do. If the device is not formatted, then Windows prompts you. Touch **Cancel**.

Figure 112.– Inserting a blank storage device

2. Open **Control Panel**. Touch **System and Security** and then touch **Administrative Tools**.

Figure 113.– Administrative Tools

3. Double-tap **Computer Management** and then touch **Disk Management**.

Chapter 7 - Connecting Peripherals

4. Touch and hold the disk that shows **Unallocated** space. Then touch **New Simple Volume**.

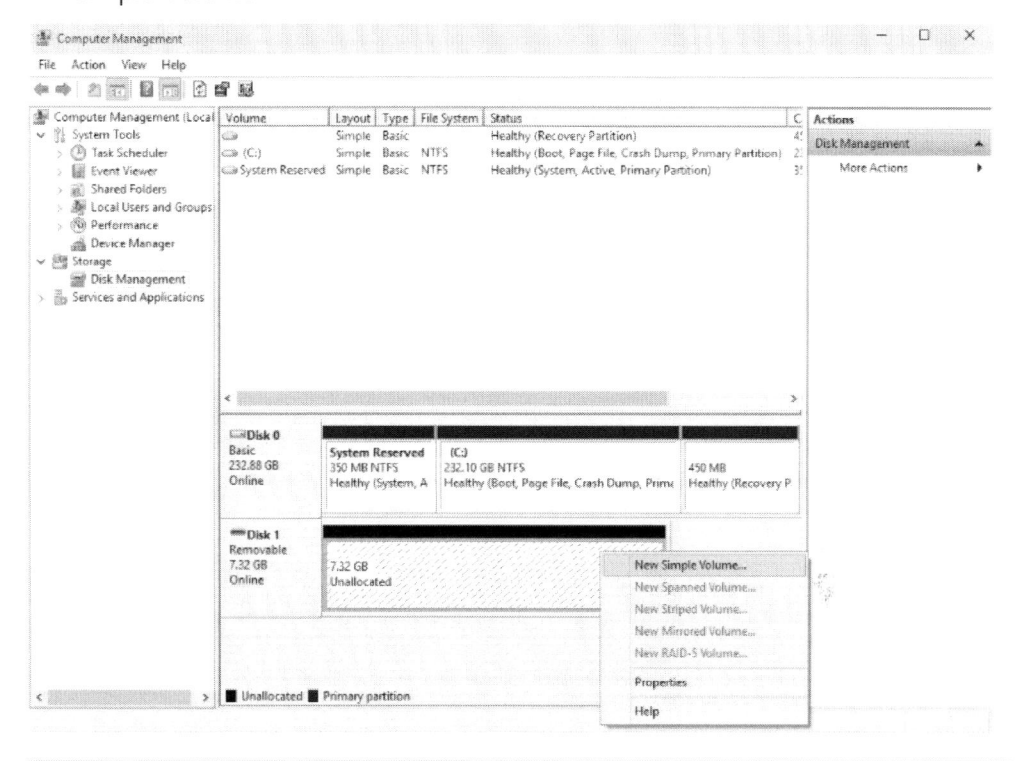

Figure 114.– Adding a new volume

5. In the **New Simple Volume Wizard**, touch **Next**.

Chapter 7 - Connecting Peripherals

6. On the **Specify Volume Size** page, touch **Next**. This results in all available space being allocated to the volume[31].

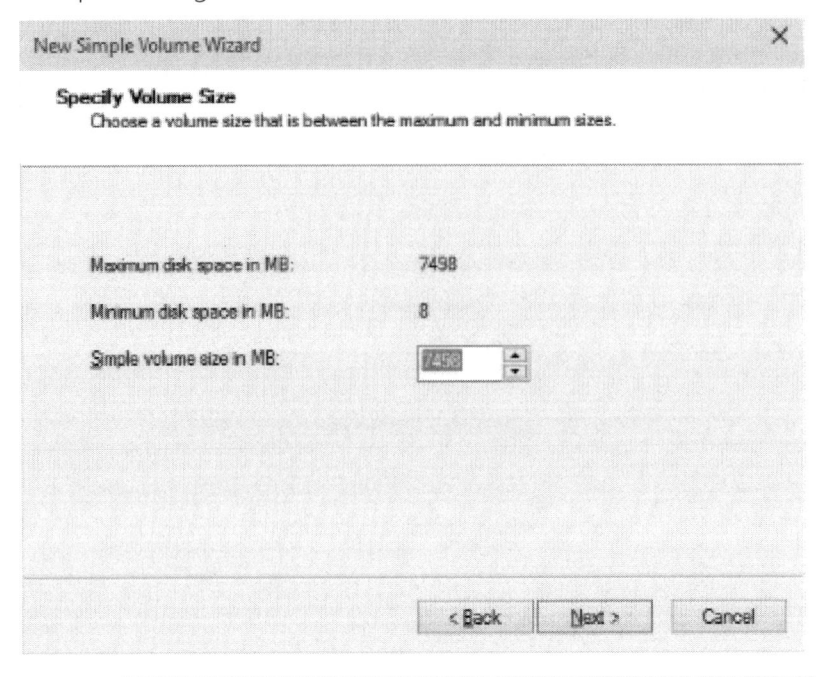

Figure 115.– Configuring the volume size

---

[31] *Volume is a Windows specific term for drive.*

Chapter 7 - Connecting Peripherals

7. On the **Assign Drive Letter or Path** page, touch **Next**. This results in the volume being assigned the next drive letter in the alphabet for use in File Explorer.

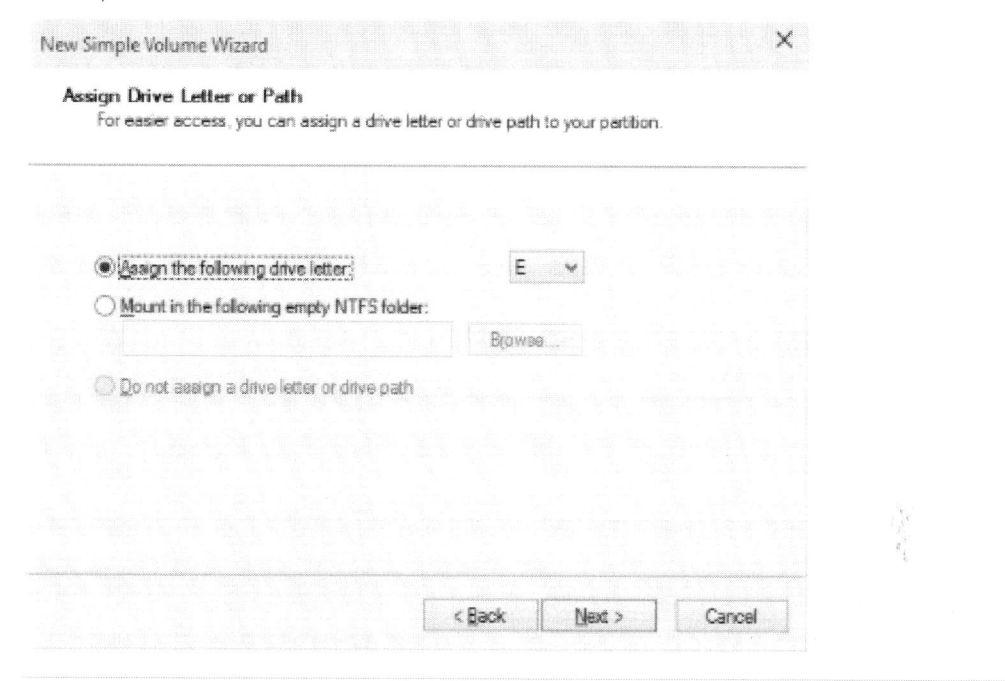

Figure 116.– Assigning a drive letter

Chapter 7 - Connecting Peripherals

8. On the **Format Partition** page, ensure that the File System is **FAT32**. Optionally, enter a volume label that describes the likely content of the volume, and then touch **Next**.

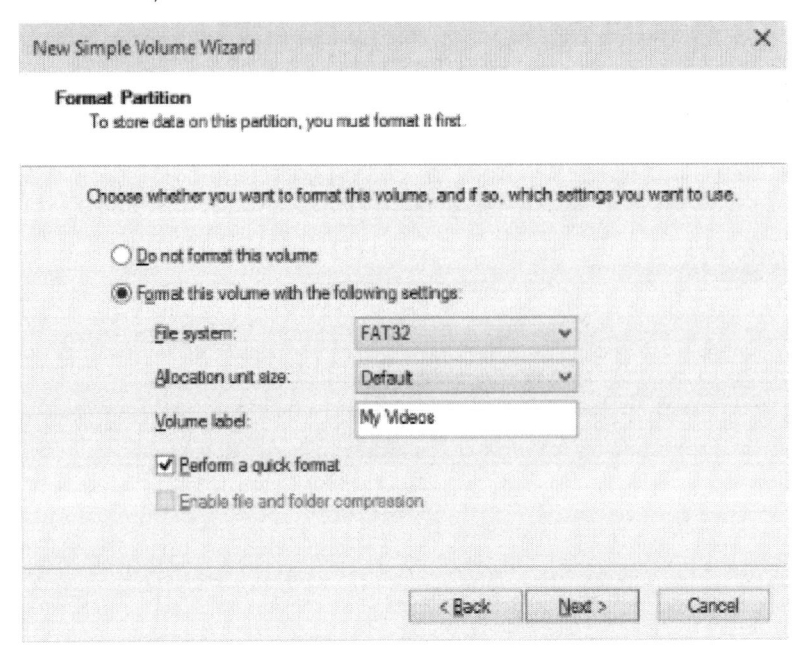

Figure 117.– Specifying the file system and volume name

Note: Using FAT32 is recommended as it is supported by most other operating systems, including Android and most media players. This means you can move the storage device around as required. Using NTFS is recommended for internal storage as it provides more security and improved reliability.

9. Touch **Finish** to complete the process. The volume is formatted and then mounted into the file system for use. You can also enable BitLocker on the drive if desired.

Chapter 7 - Connecting Peripherals

When removing storage drives, it is good practice to use the option to safely remove the device. To do this, from the system tray, touch and hold the **Safely Remove Hardware and Eject Media** icon and then touch **Eject** *storage*. Failure to do this can result in media corruption.

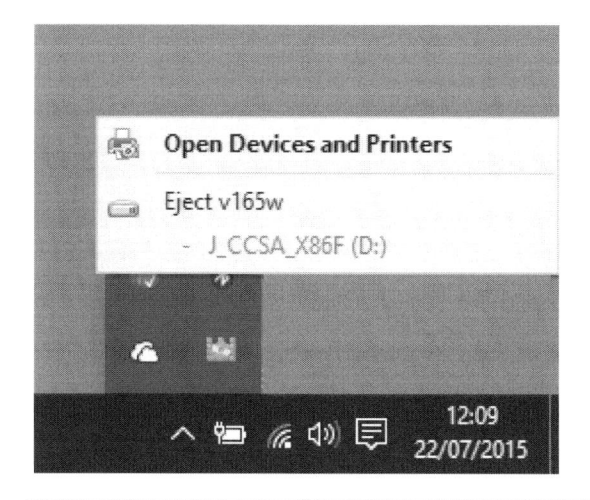

Figure 118.– Ejecting a storage device

Chapter 7 - Connecting Peripherals

This page left intentionally blank

Chapter 8

Troubleshooting and Recovery

What you will do in this chapter:

- Configure Windows Update settings
- Learn how to back up your device
- Explore recovery options

Windows Update

It is very important to keep Windows 10 up to date. By doing so, you ensure that any security flaws can be addressed, and additional functions added to the operating system are available to you[32]. In corporate networks, a centralized file server is often used to distribute updates to client devices, but in a home network, the responsibility of managing updates rests with you.

Configuring Windows Update

Windows Update is the internal update manager in Windows 10. You can configure Windows Update behaviour from **Settings**. Choose **Update & security** and then touch **Windows Update**.

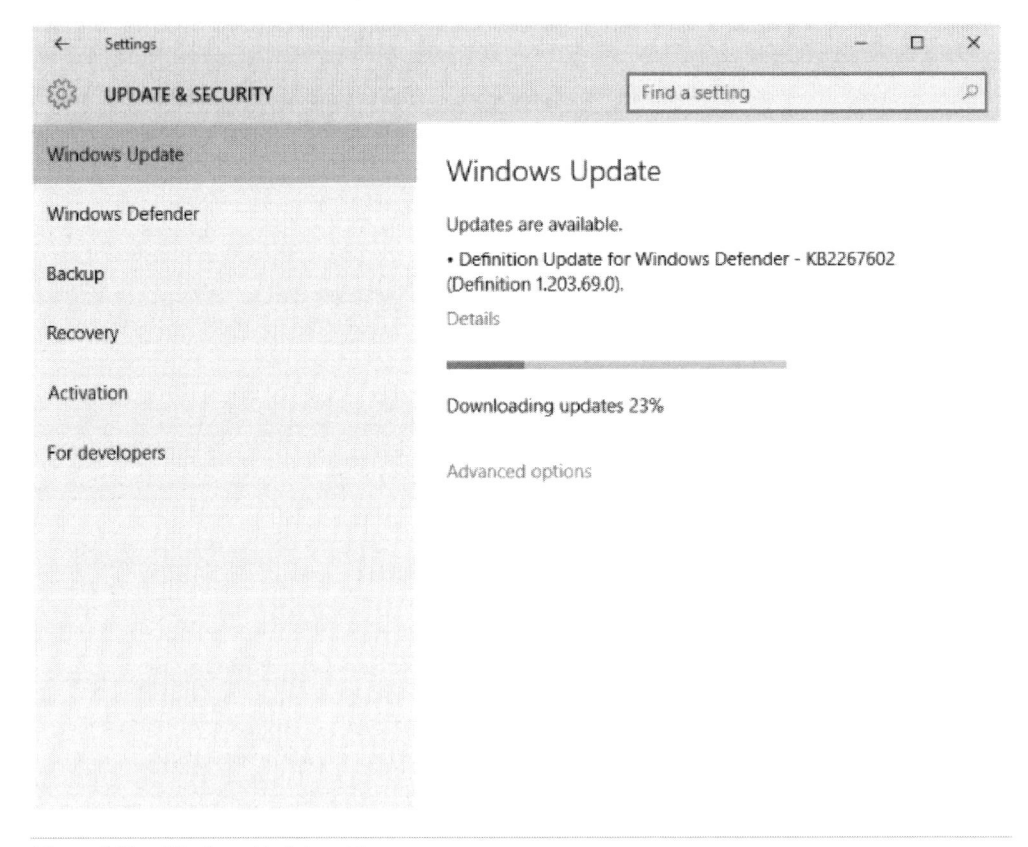

Figure 119.– Windows Update settings

---

[32] *At the time of writing, Microsoft have indicated that they do not intend to produce major operating system updates from now on, instead relying on Windows Update to deliver a constant stream of updates as the platform develops.*

Chapter 8 - Troubleshooting and Recovery

You can view the update status, and you can select **Advanced options** to control how updates are applied to your device.

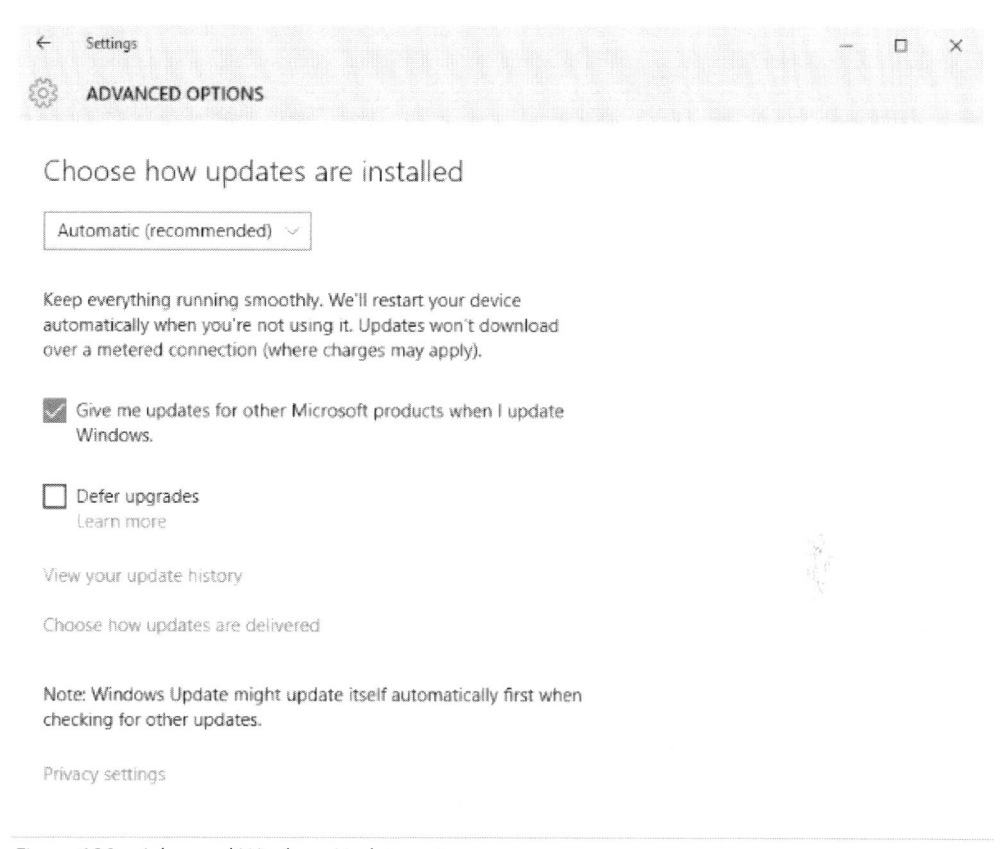

Figure 120.– Advanced Windows Update options

From this window, you can:

- **Choose how updates are installed.** Enables you to choose between **Automatic (recommended)** and **Notify to schedule restart**.

- **Give me updates for other Microsoft products when I update Windows.** This ensures that software and apps, such as Microsoft Office, are updated when Windows is updated.

- **Defer upgrades.** Microsoft use Windows Update to deliver additional features to Windows in addition to minor updates and fixes. These more significant feature updates can be deferred by selecting this option.

Chapter 8 - Troubleshooting and Recovery

- **View your update history**. Enables you to see which updates have been applied. You can choose to uninstall updates from here. You can also determine why an update didn't install. Touch the detail beneath an update for further information.

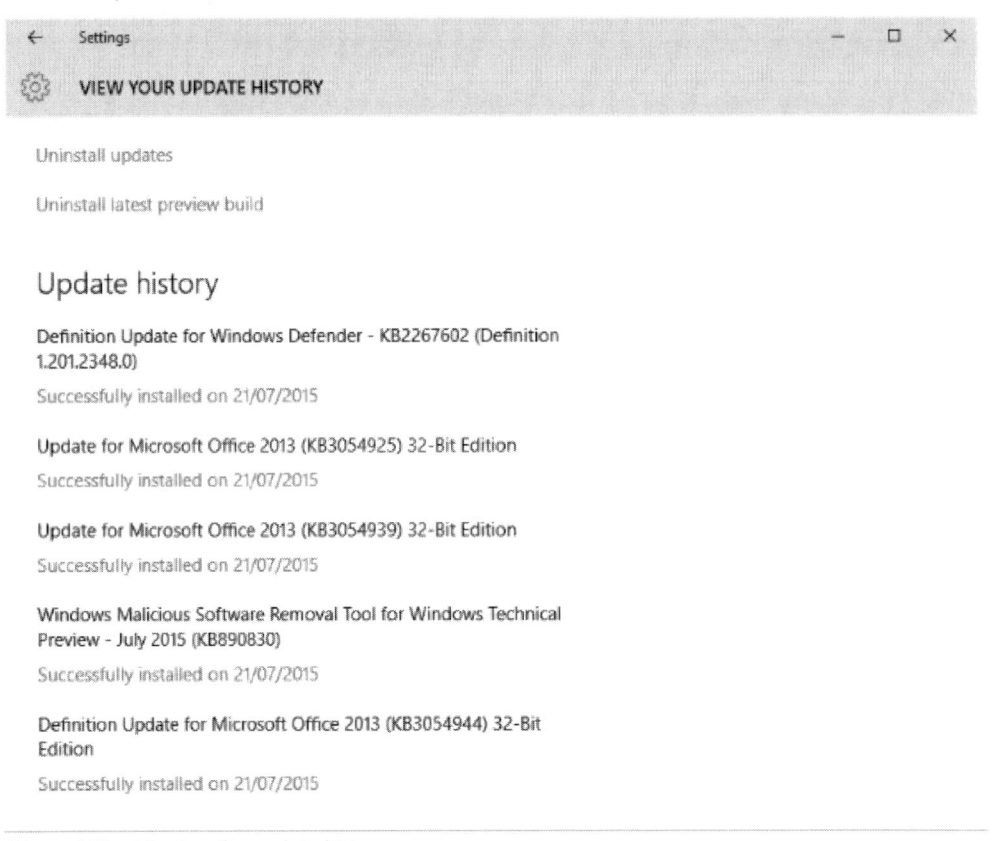

Figure 121.— Viewing the update history

Chapter 8 - Troubleshooting and Recovery

- **Choose how updates are delivered.** You can enable the ability for Windows to download updates from multiple sources. This increases the speed of update download.

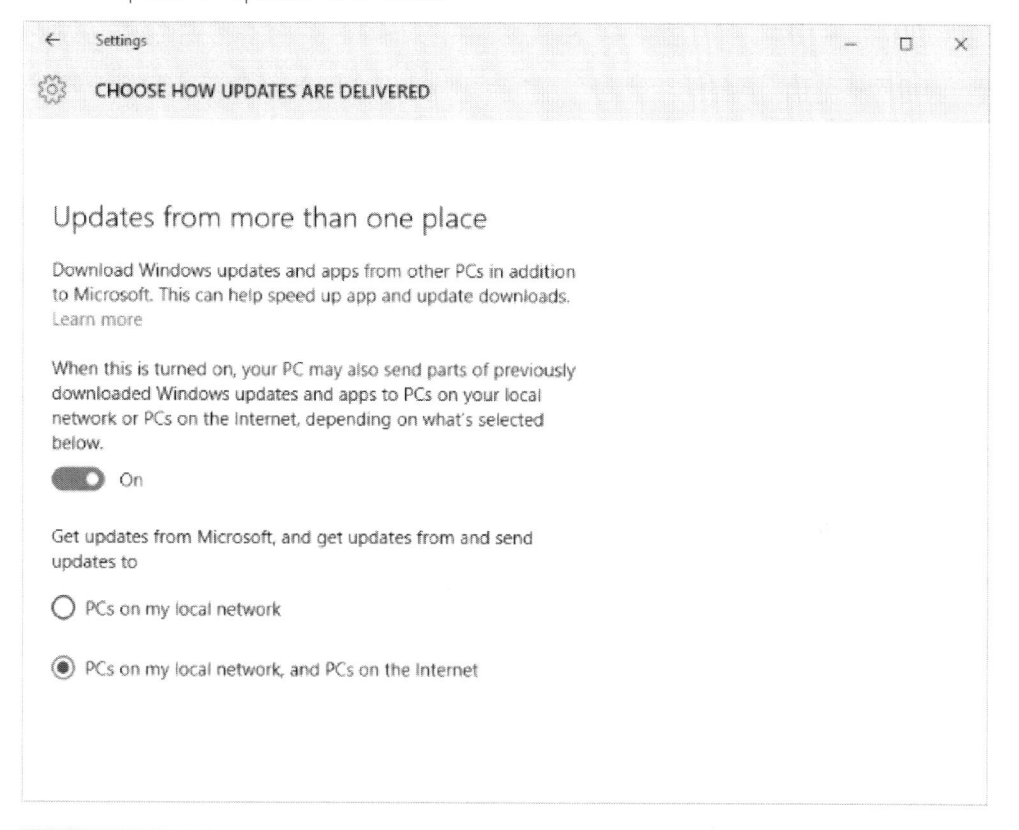

Figure 122.– Choosing how to deliver updates

Generally, you will not need to make changes to the way Windows handles updates as the default configuration is the best way to obtain updates and maintain the integrity of your Windows device.

The Importance of Backup

Although Windows is a reliable operating system, stuff can still go wrong. It's all too easy to lose files either through a device failure or through file corruption of accidental deletion. That's why it's important to back up your data files.

I have always been a believer in keeping multiple copies of important files, especially those I am working on in active projects. It's deeply frustrating to lose your work, and to have to try to remember what was lost and to recreate it. At any one time, I would normally have four versions of a file in various locations. Belt, braces, and more belts.

Using Backup and Restore (Windows 7)

To provide for a degree of backwards compatibility, Windows 10 includes a tool familiar to those of you who have used Windows 7 – the Backup and Restore tool. I would urge you to use the tools developed for Windows 10 discussed later in this lesson. However, you can access this legacy tool from **Control Panel** or from **Settings**.

1. In **Settings**, touch **Update & security**, and then touch **Backup**.

2. In the results pane, touch **Go to Backup and Restore (Windows 7)**.

3. Touch **Set up back-up**.

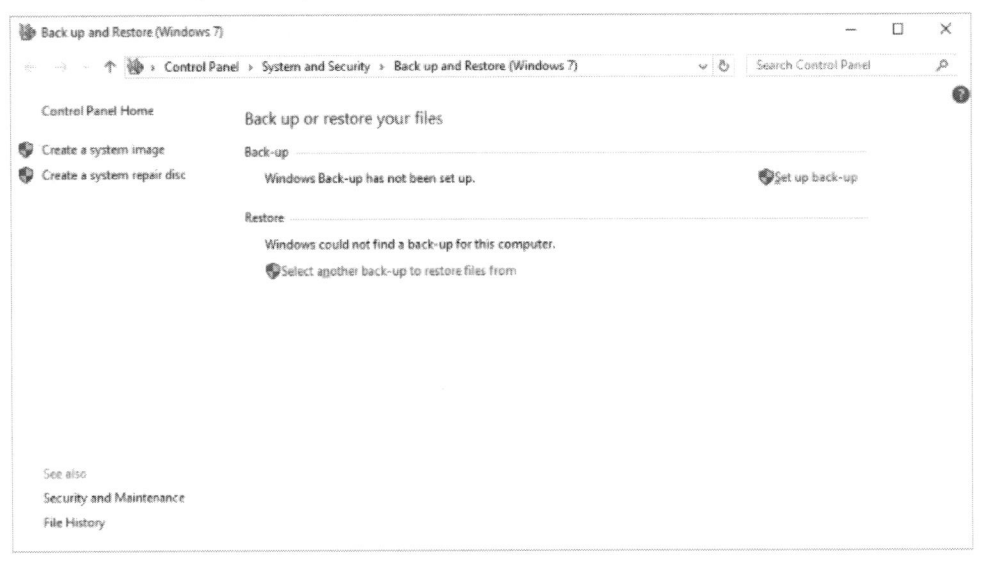

Figure 123.– Initialising Backup and Restore (Windows 7)

Chapter 8 - Troubleshooting and Recovery

4. You must then specify a location to which you wish to backup. Clearly, that must be a different disk – either a removable disk, or a storage area on a network server. Select an appropriate drive and touch **Next**.

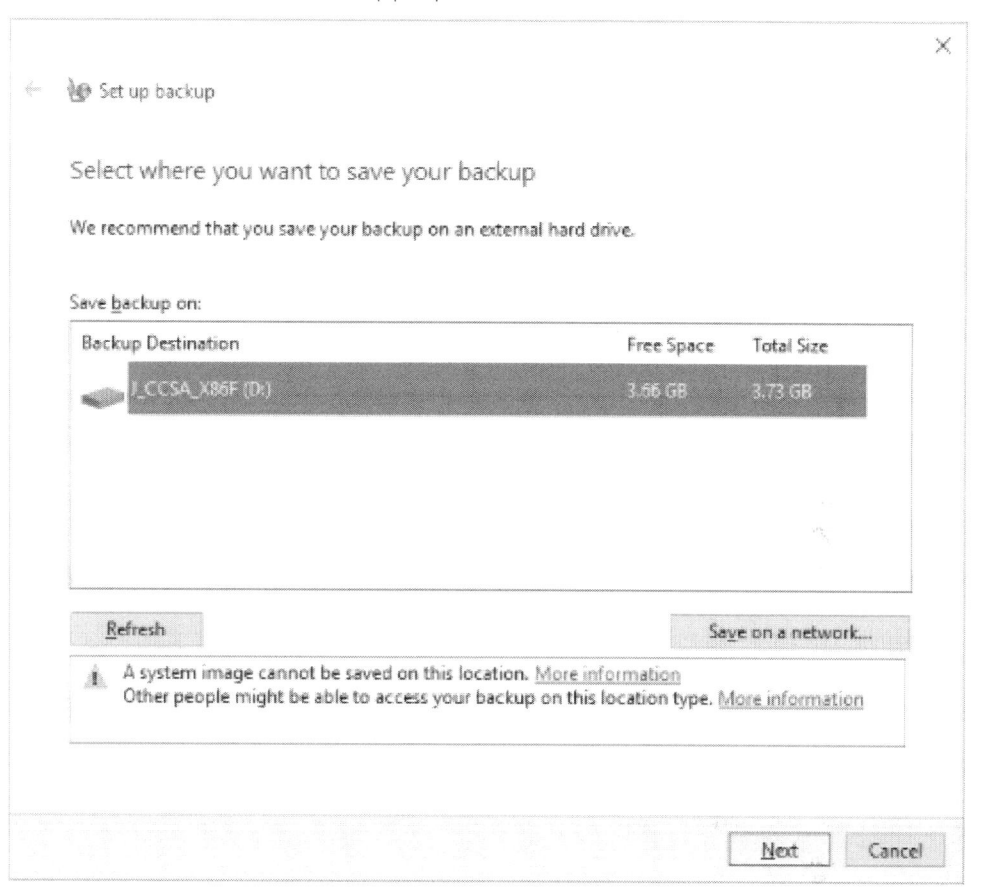

Figure 124.– Selecting a suitable backup drive

Chapter 8 - Troubleshooting and Recovery

5. Choose what to back up. Select between **Let Windows choose**, or **Let me choose**. If you opt for the latter, you must specify where the files are that you want to protect. Generally, let Windows choose and then touch **Next**.

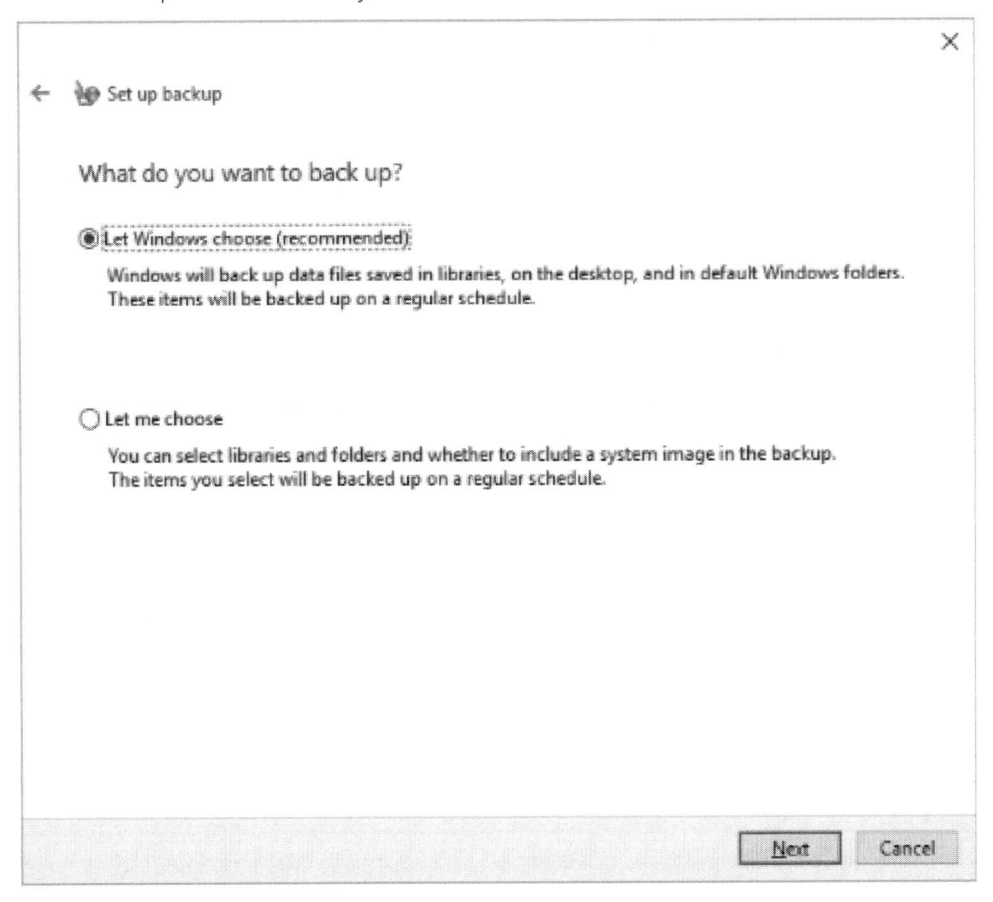

Figure 125.– Select what to backup

Chapter 8 - Troubleshooting and Recovery

6. On the **Review your backup settings** page, you can specify a schedule by touching **Change schedule**. When you are ready, touch **Save settings and run backup**.

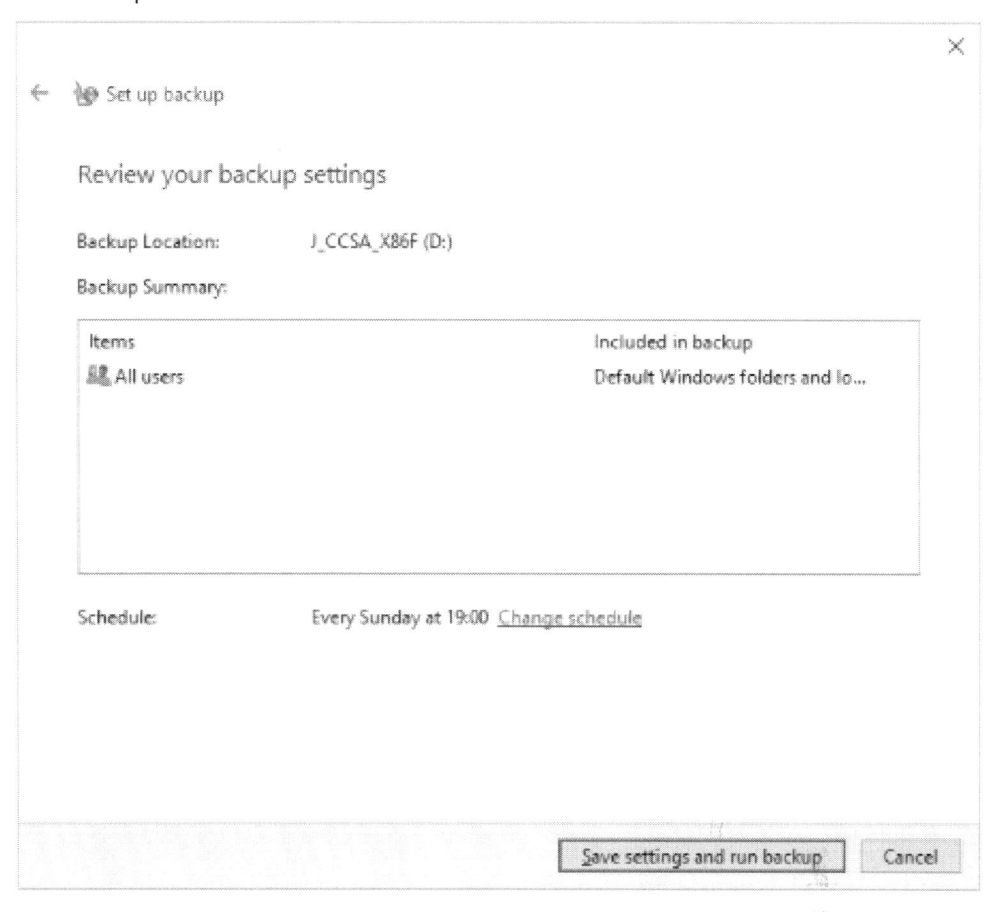

Figure 126.– Save settings

Backup and Restore (Windows 7) also enables you to create a **System Image** and a **System Repair Disc**. If you create either of these, the resultant backups can be used to recover the Windows 10 device in certain situations.

- A **system image** backup is a backup of the drives required to enable Windows to run. It is a complete duplicate on your hard drives. You can back up the system image to a removable hard disk, to a writeable DVD, or to a network location.

- A **system repair disc** is used to startup your computer in the event that the startup files become corrupted. You must have a writeable CD/DVD drive in your device to use this tool.

Chapter 8 - Troubleshooting and Recovery

Using File History

Aside from manually copying important files, you can also use the File History tool provided in Windows 10 to help to protect your data. You can access this tool from **Control Panel**. Touch **System and Security** and then touch **File History**.

Note: For File History to work, you must have an additional drive to store your data backups. This drive can be on a network, or it can be local. I recommend going to a computer store and buying an inexpensive external hard disk that can be connected to your device for this purpose. However, for tablet devices, this is probably impractical.

Assuming you have an additional local drive attached, to setup File History:

1. Touch **Turn on**. That's it. Your files, stored in your libraries and including your contacts and web browser favourites, are all backed up to the device.

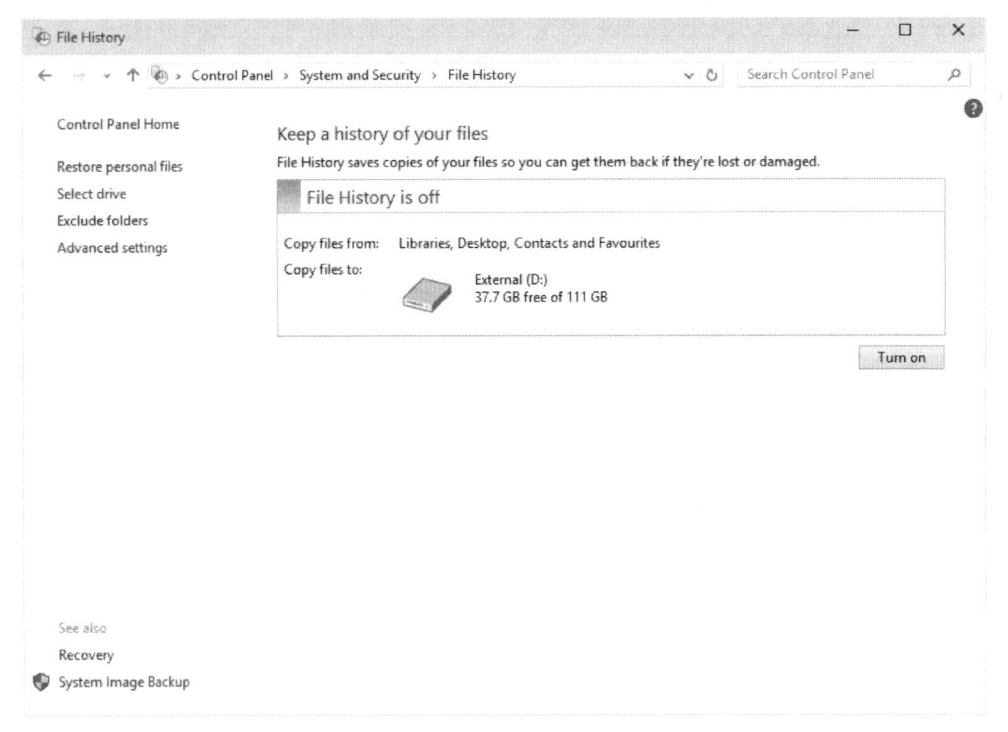

Figure 127.– Enabling File History

Note: Your files are backed up into a folder called **FileHistory** on the volume selected for backup.

To restore files by using File History:

1. Open **File History** from Control Panel.
2. Touch **Restore personal files**.

Chapter 8 - Troubleshooting and Recovery

3. In the **Home – File History** window, all your backed up data is displayed. Select the folder(s) you want to restore.

Figure 128.– Selecting folder(s) to restore

4. If you want to restore an individual file, browse for its location and then select that file.

Figure 129.– Selecting a file for restoration

Chapter 8 - Troubleshooting and Recovery

5. You can use the left and right arrow keys to navigate between versions of the backup.

Figure 130.– The navigation bar

6. When you are ready to restore a file(s) or folder(s), touch the **Restore** button. If the file exists in the restore location, you are prompted. Touch **Copy and Replace** unless you want to keep both the current and restored versions. File Explorer opens on the restoration location. Your file(s) or folder(s) is restored.

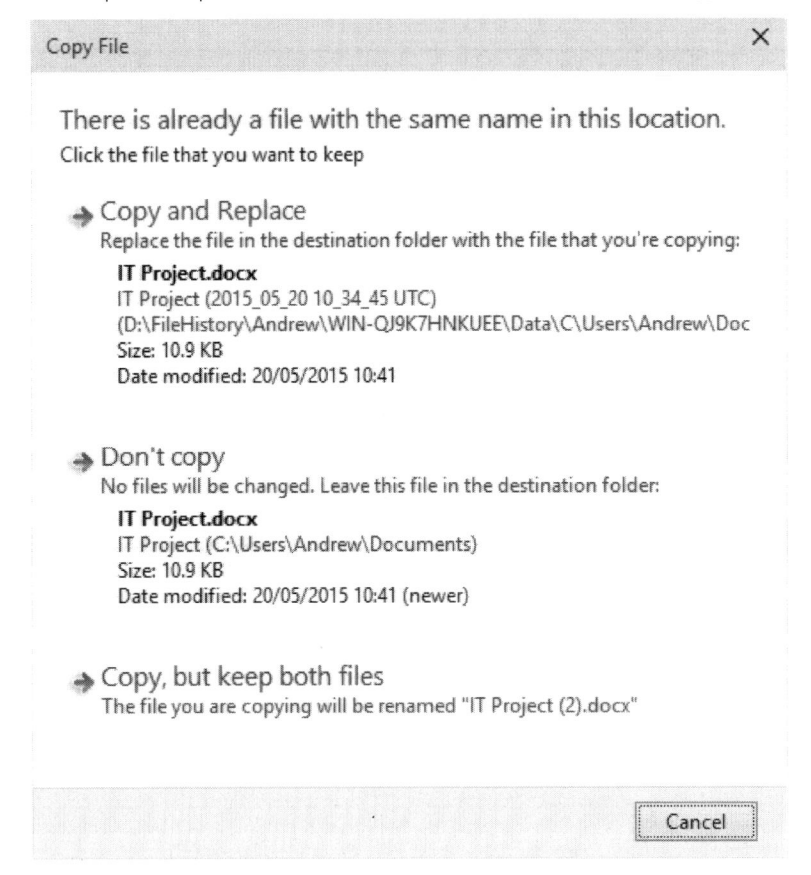

Figure 131.– Choosing how to restore the file

Note: If you want to restore to an alternate location, use the **Options** button and touch **Restore To**.

Chapter 8 - Troubleshooting and Recovery

Using Previous Versions to restore files

Previous Versions is a Windows file recovery feature that is available when you have enabled system protection[33] on a volume. You can use Previous Versions to restore a file to a previous version. If you deleted the file, you can recover the deleted file by restoring the folder that contains the deleted file back to a point in time when the file existed.

Note: You should exercise caution when restoring a whole folder as the other contents of the folder may be affected. It is typical to restore the folder to an alternate location and then manually moving the recovered file.

To restore a file to a previous version:

1. Open **File Explorer** and navigate to the folder that contains the file.
2. Touch and hold the file and then touch **Properties**.

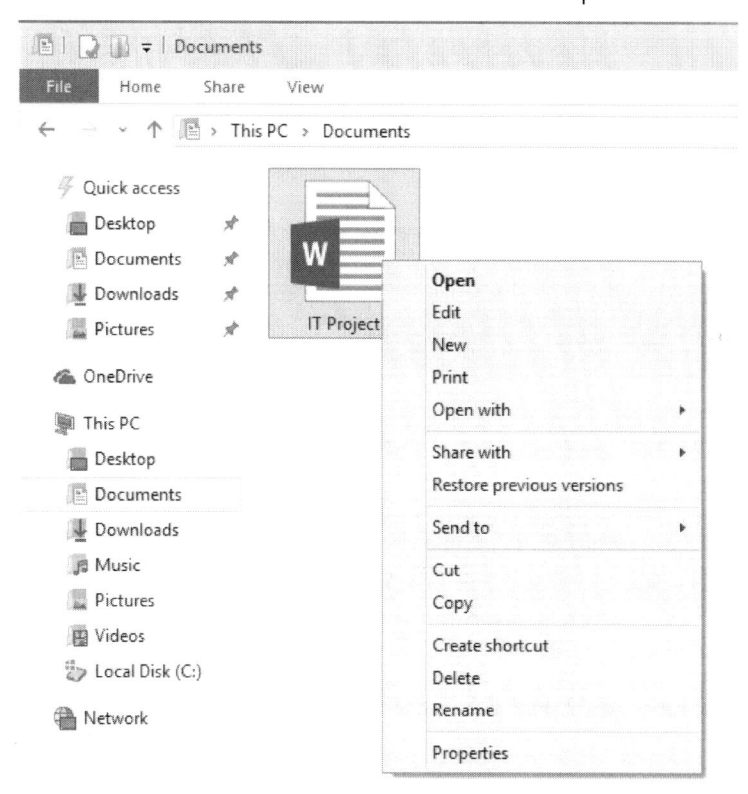

Figure 132.– Opening file properties

---

[33] *System protection creates snapshots of your Windows device's configuration – but additionally creates copies of data files on protected volumes. System protection is enabled by default on the system volume.*

Page - 157

Chapter 8 - Troubleshooting and Recovery

3. In the *file* **Properties** window, touch the **Previous Versions** tab.

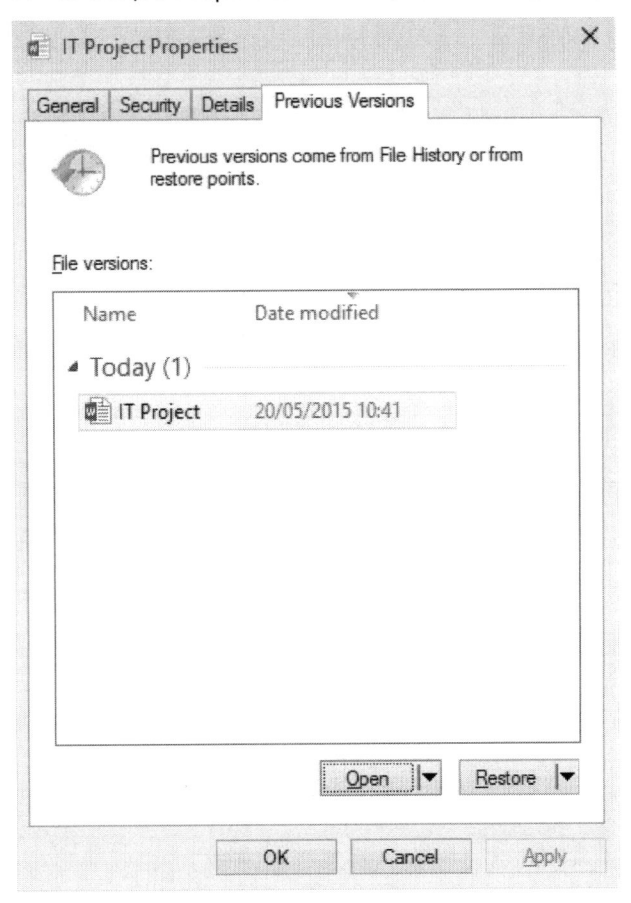

Figure 133.– Previous Versions tab

4. You can see previous versions of the file listed. Select the appropriate version and then touch **Restore**. If you want to restore the file to an alternate location, touch the arrow to the right of Restore and then touch **Restore To**. Then browse and select a suitable location. You can manually copy the restored file to its proper location later.

Chapter 8 - Troubleshooting and Recovery

5. When prompted, touch **Restore** to complete the process.

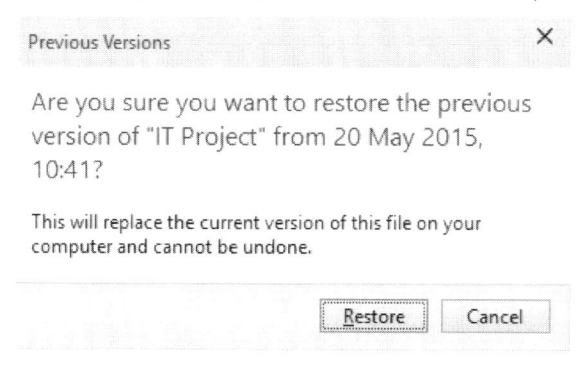

Figure 134.– Restoring a file using a previous version

6. Touch **OK** twice to close open windows.

Note: To enable system protection, see the next section.

Recovery Options in Windows 10

Windows 10 is a robust, reliable operating system. Even so, from time to time, you may experience problems caused by an unreliable driver, a defective software component, or an update that conflicts with other system components. Luckily, built in to the operating system are features that you can use to help recover from these and other problems that you might experience.

These recovery features include:

- **Driver rollback.** All hardware components within your device require a device driver. Windows uses this device driver to interact with the hardware. If you install an updated driver and then experience reliability issues with that device, or other components within the system, you can use driver rollback to attempt to resolve the problem. You can access driver rollback from **Device Manager**.

- **System protection.** System protection creates snapshots of your Windows device's configuration. These snapshots are taken periodically, and before significant configuration changes are made to your device. You can then use system protection to revert the configuration of your device to a previous point-in-time[34]. You can access system protection from the **System** properties in **Control Panel**.

- **Recovery modes.** Windows 10 includes two recovery modes. You can access these modes from **Update & security** in **Settings**. The recovery modes are:

    o **Reset this PC.** If you want to rollback to an earlier configuration, and the preceding two recovery features were unsuccessful, you can use this option. It is fairly invasive in that it reinstalls the operating system. However, you have the option to either remove everything (in essence, rebuilding your device from scratch), or else you can select to retain your personal files.

    o **Advanced startup.** This option launches a special startup environment that enables you to choose between a variety of recovery options. It is also the launch platform for some of the preceding recovery modes.

When considering the use of these tools, you should be aware that although they might help you recover from the specific problem you are experiencing with your

---

[34] *System protection also enables file recovery through a feature called Previous versions.*

Chapter 8 - Troubleshooting and Recovery

Windows device, they may also have other less desirable side-effects. Always try to use the least invasive, least destructive recovery method for any situation. In other words, if you just updated a driver, use driver rollback before you use system restore. If you have a more serious problem, try system restore before resorting to a refresh.

Creating restore points with System Protection

System protection enables you to recover you device to a configuration point in time. It also enables Previous Versions for file recovery. To enable system protection and create a restore point, use the following procedure:

1. Open **Control Panel**.
2. Touch **System and Security** and then touch **System**.
3. In the System window, touch **System protection**.

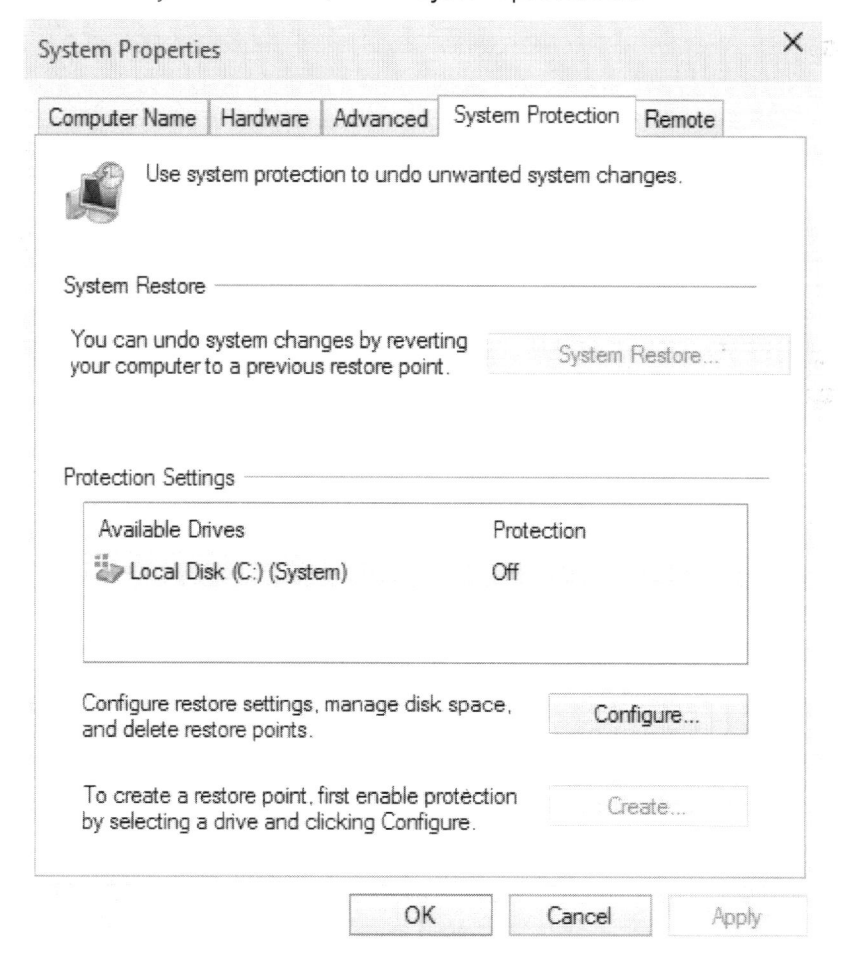

Figure 135.– System Protection window

Page - 161

Chapter 8 - Troubleshooting and Recovery

4. If your system drive is not already enabled for protection, touch **Configure**.

5. In the **System Protection for Local Disk (C:)** window, touch **Turn on system protection** and then touch **OK**.

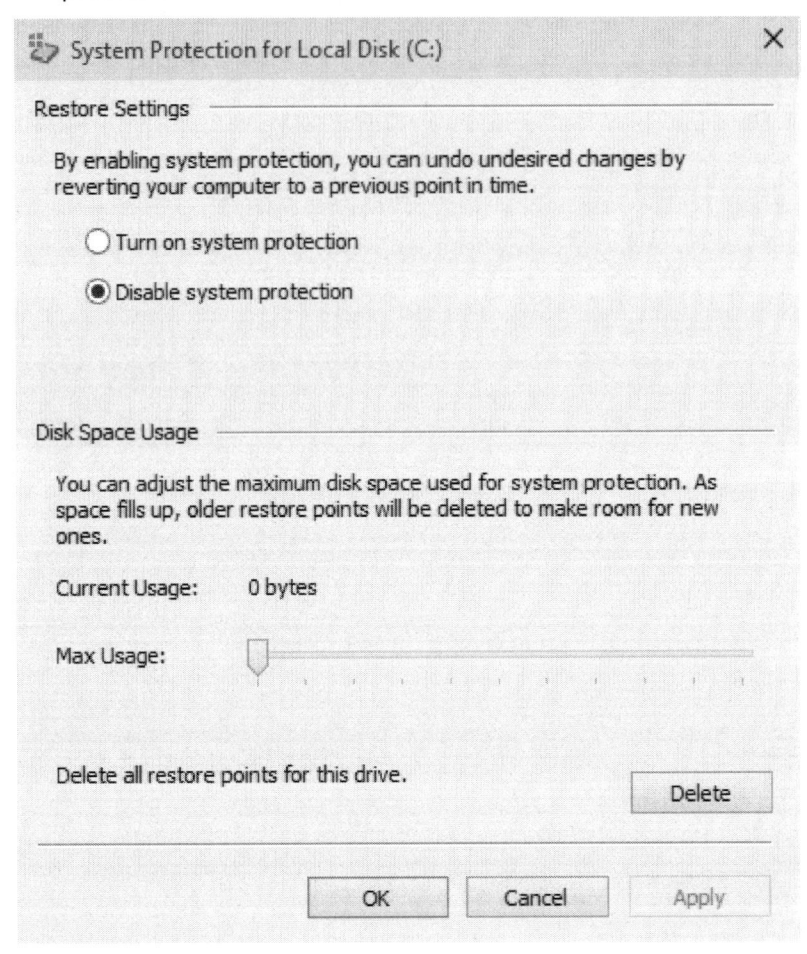

Figure 136.– Enabling System Protection

6. To create a restore point, in the **System Properties** window, touch **Create**.

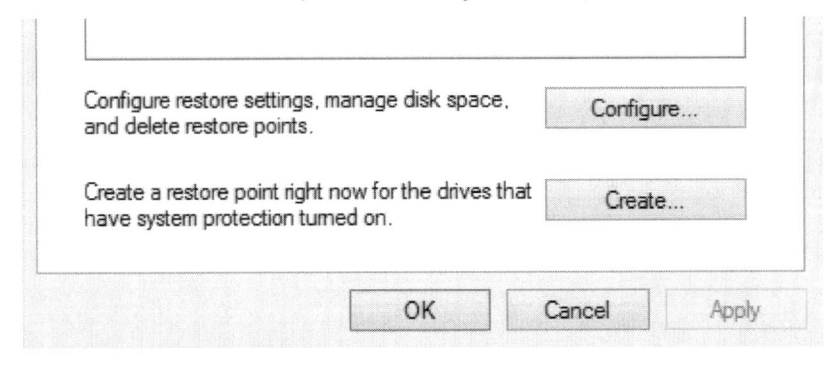

Figure 137.– Create a restore point

Page - 162

Chapter 8 - Troubleshooting and Recovery

7. In the **System Protection** window, type a name for your restore point. If you are about to install a new app, or updates some drivers, then type a name descriptive of that. Then touch **Create**. The restore point is created.

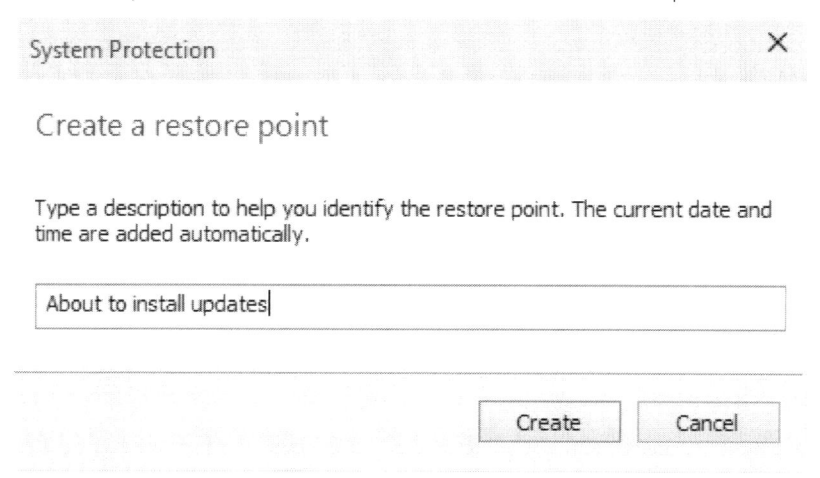

Figure 138.– Naming the restore point

Note: Windows creates restore points automatically on a scheduled basis, and also before any significant system configuration changes. However, I would always recommend creating one yourself before any major changes are implemented on your device.

8. Touch **Close** when the restore point is completed.

Using a restore point to revert to a previous system configuration

Using a restore point restores the entire system configuration of your device to the selected point in time. Any changes from that point onwards are lost. Typically, after applying a restore point, you would expect to see Windows Update applying previously applied updates to get your device up to date.

Note: Your data files are not affected by a system restore.

Chapter 8 - Troubleshooting and Recovery

If you must recover the configuration from a previous restore point, then:

1. From within the **System Properties** window, touch **System Restore**.

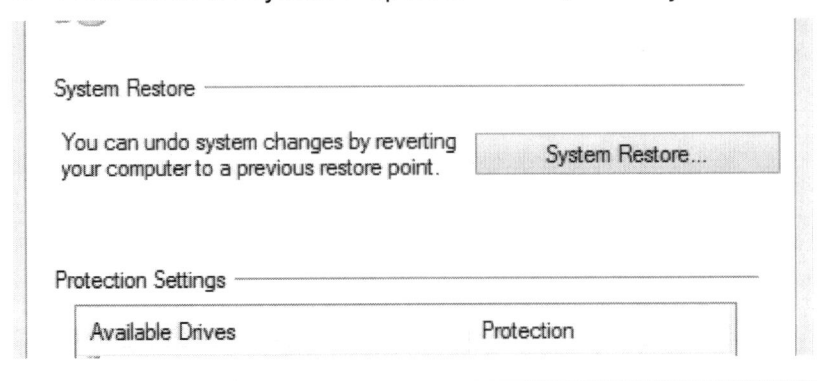

Figure 139.– Starting a system restore

2. The **System Restore** wizard launches. Touch **Next**.

3. On the **Restore your computer to the state it was in before the selected event** page, touch the restore point you want and then touch **Next**.

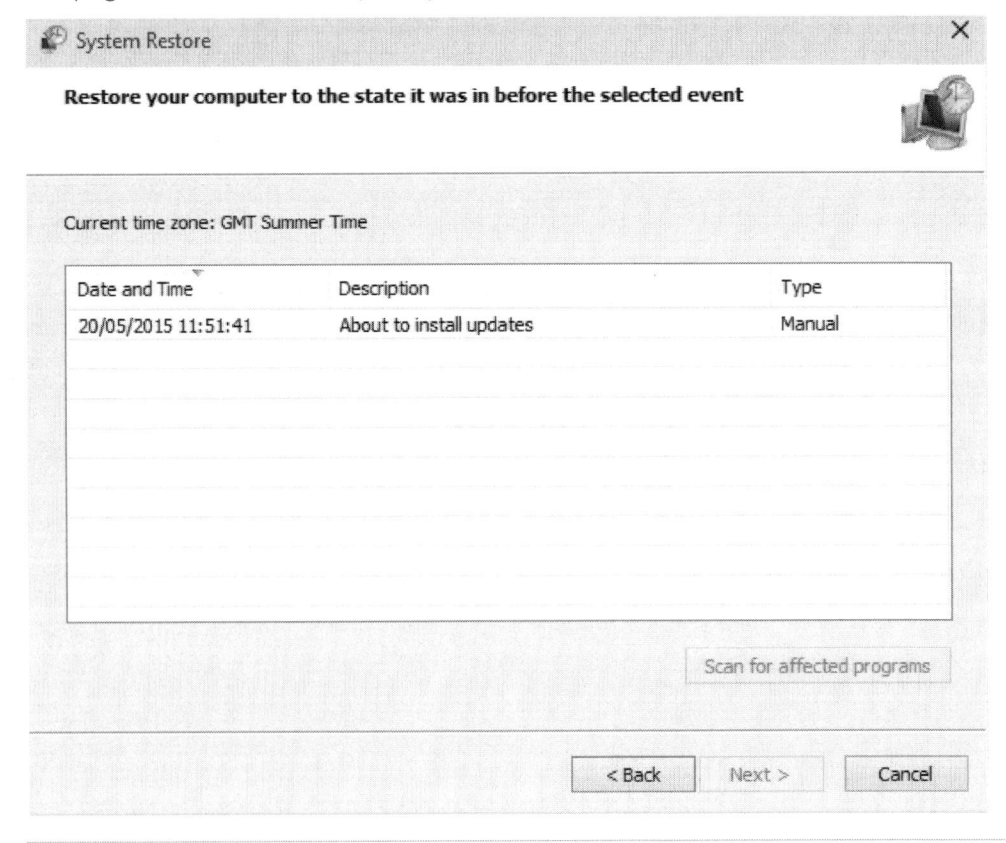

Figure 140.– Selecting a restore point

Chapter 8 - Troubleshooting and Recovery

4. On the **Confirm your restore point** page, touch **Finish** to complete the process. Your device will restart during the process. When finished, sign in using your Microsoft account.

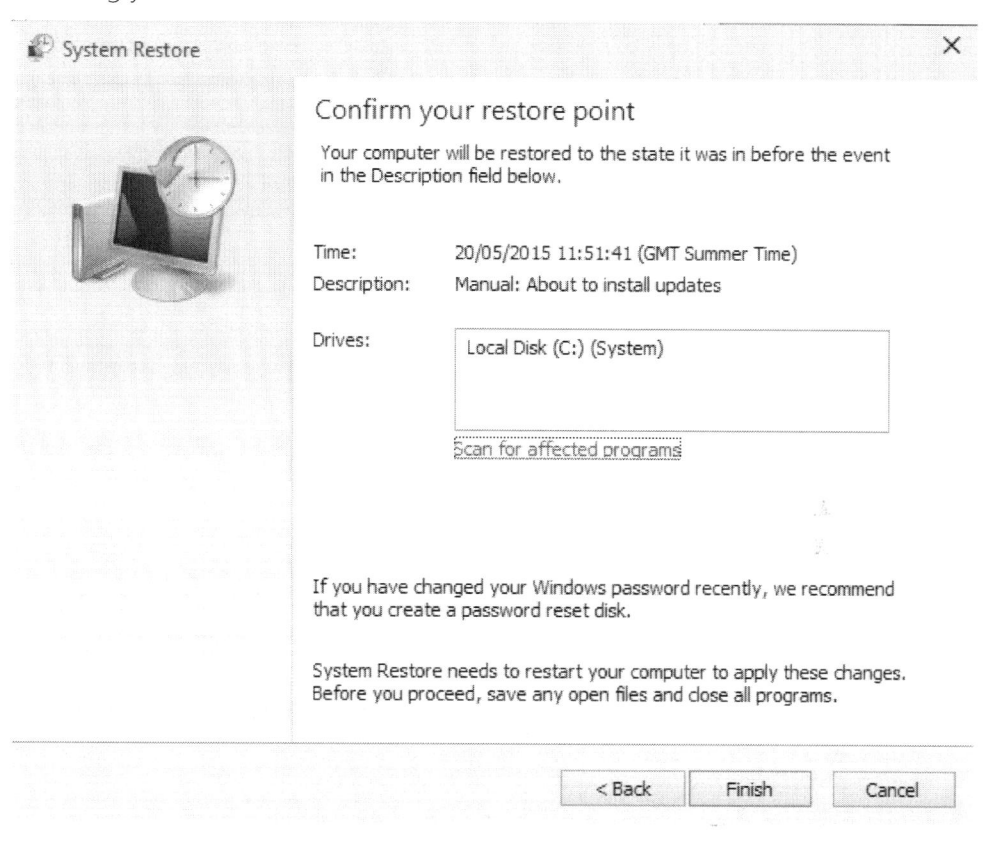

Figure 141.– Confirming the restore

If you decide that was the wrong restore point, you can undo this operation when you first sign in – you are prompted to revert the system restore upon sign in. Alternatively, you can manually choose another restore point.

Using Advanced Startup

The Advanced startup options enable you to try other recovery modes. These are:

- **Use a device.** You can start from a version of Windows to Go or some troubleshooting tool that you have installed on a DVD or USB storage device.

- **Troubleshoot.** Enables you to perform Refresh or Reset operations on your device, and also to access:

  o **Reset this PC.** This enables you to remove and reinstall Windows – optionally keeping your personal files if you wish. Note, all your apps are removed, so this is not an option to consider if you have any other way to recover your device.

  o **Advanced startup.** A number of recovery options are available. These are discussed below.

How to access Advanced startup

The following procedure assumes that you can start your device in the first place. If this is not the case, then you must startup in System Recovery mode. You can access this from a Windows tablet by pressing a combination of the physical buttons on device. The specifics of this vary from device to device, but on my Lenovo, I press and hold the Volume Up button and then press and release the Power button[35]. I see a menu that displays a number of options, including System Recovery. It is this last option you need. Proceed from step 3 below.

---

[35] *If you use a PC or laptop, then you may need to press keyboard keys to activate the recovery startup menu. These vary from vendor to vendor, but usually the function keys are used. You may need to search the Internet to discover which key to use, but my HP laptop uses F10.*

Chapter 8 - Troubleshooting and Recovery

To launch Advanced startup from within Windows:

1. From **Settings**, touch **Update & security**.
2. Touch **Recovery** and then, under Advanced Startup, touch **Restart now**.

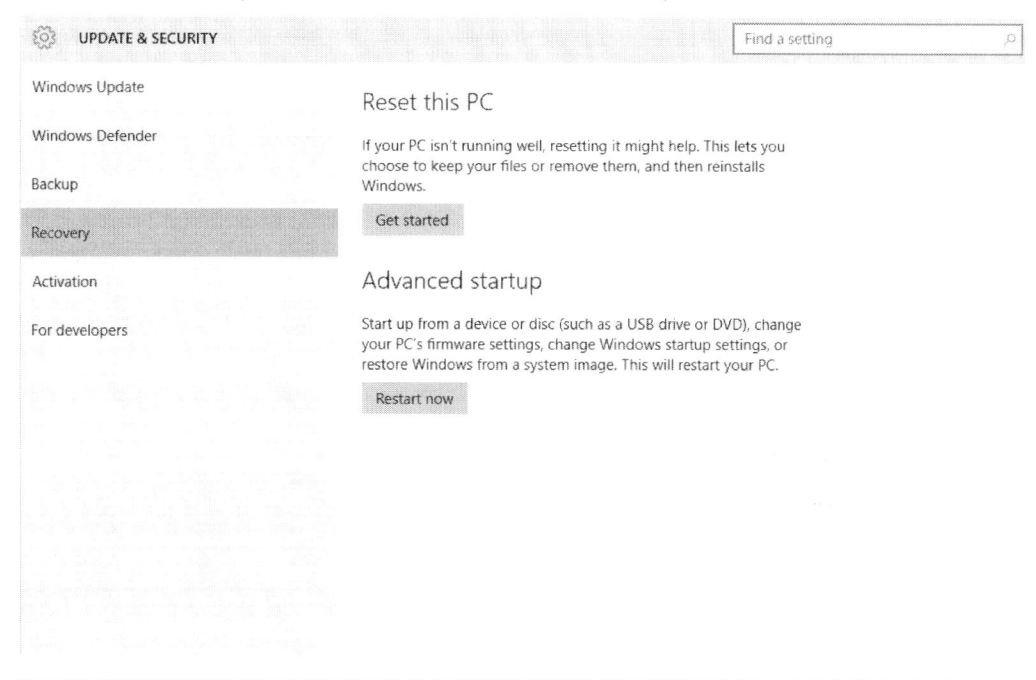

Figure 142.– Launching Advanced startup

3. Your device restarts into Advanced startup mode.

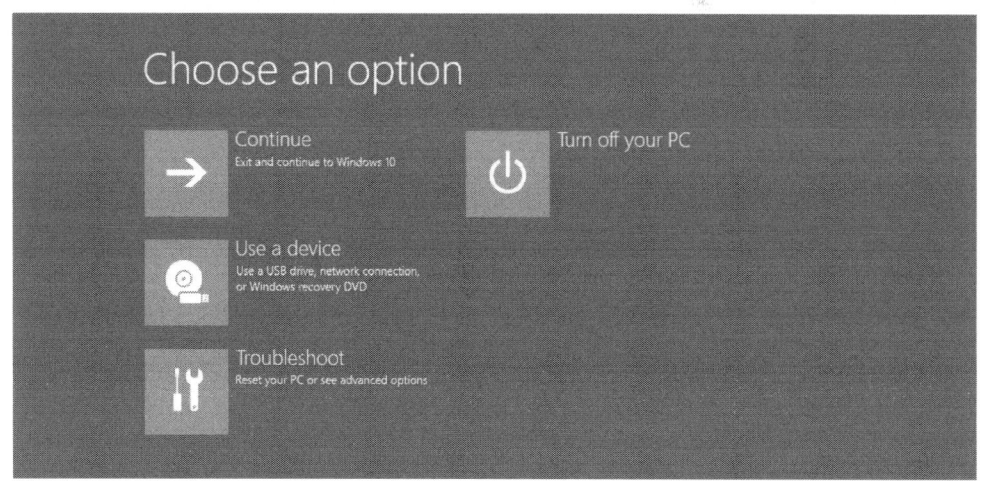

Figure 143.– Choose an option

4. At the **Choose an option** page, touch **Troubleshoot**.

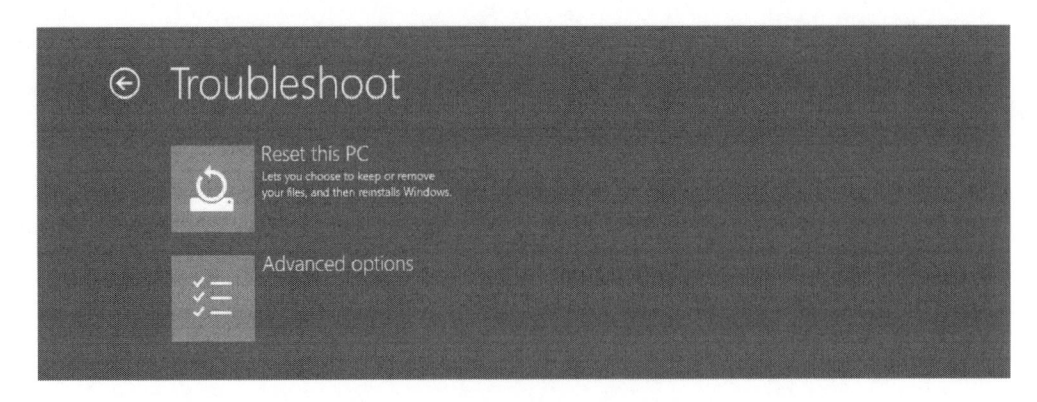

Figure 144.– Troubleshoot options

5. At the **Troubleshoot** page, touch **Advanced options**.

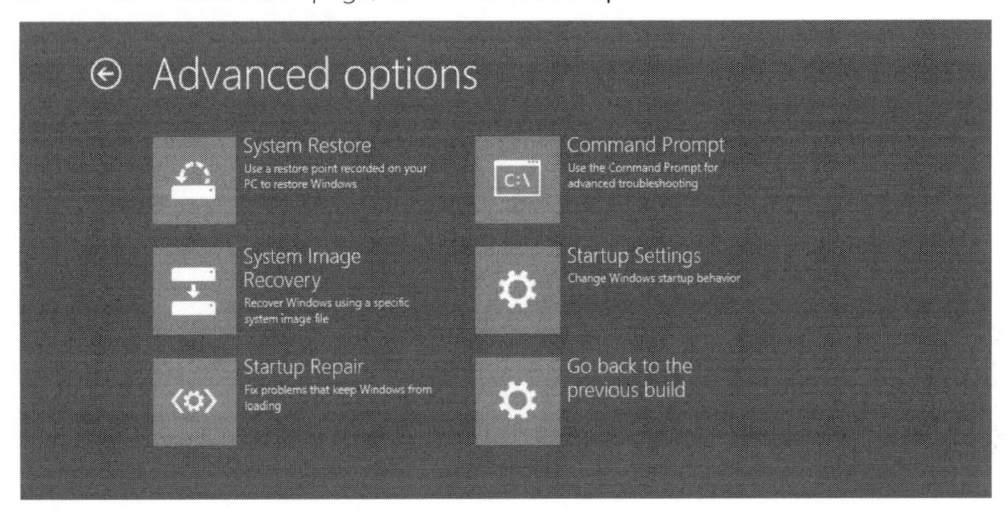

Figure 145.– Advanced options

Advanced options provide the following tools:

- **System Restore.** You can select and apply restore points from here. The process is similar to the process used within Windows.

- **System Recovery Image.** If you have created a complete system image backup, use this option to restore it now. Create your system image backup using the Backup and Restore (Windows 7) tool.

- **Startup Repair.** When Windows won't start, it can be because of one of a number of issues, including damaged or missing device drivers, corrupt configuration store (known as the registry), missing startup files (known also as boot files), and other possibilities. This tool enables you to easily

Chapter 8 - Troubleshooting and Recovery

diagnose, and where possible, automatically repair common startup problems.

- **Command Prompt**. Very much an advanced user tool, the command prompt enables you to enter commands at a text-only window. These commands enable you to manually perform startup diagnostics and repair, examine and replace device drivers, and interact with the storage configuration of your device. Leave this option unless you have specific instructions on what to do.

- **Startup Settings**. Windows can be started, or booted, using one-off startup settings. These settings change the behaviour of Windows startup so that you can perform diagnostic investigation of problems with your device. Startup Settings options include:

    o **Low-resolution video mode** for when you suspect a video driver is your problem.

    o **Debugging mode** to enable an engineer to remotely connect to your device to diagnose internal operating system behaviour.

    o **Boot logging mode**, so that you can check what happens during startup.

    o **Safe mode**, which launches Windows in a minimal state with as much turned off as possible. From this state, you may be able to recover Windows using a restore point.

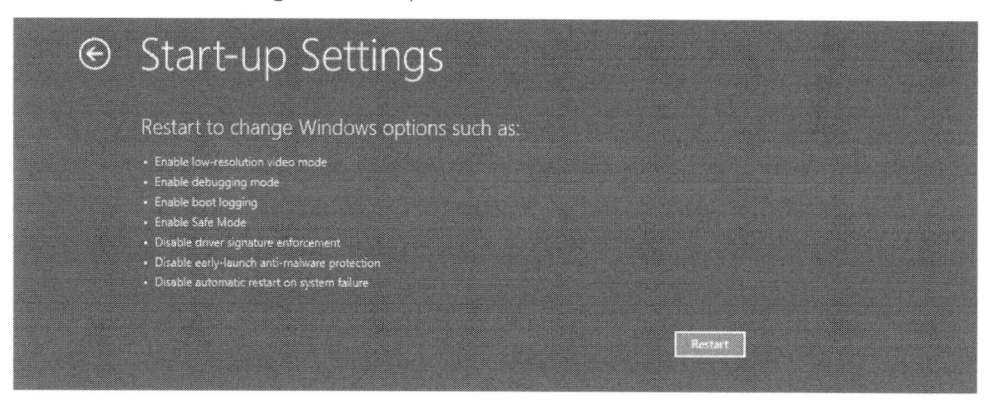

Figure 146.– Startup Settings options

When you have finished whichever procedure you have attempted, you are prompted to restart your device. With luck, the problem is resolved. If not, you must attempt another resolution method.

Recovery partitions

It's worth noting that most vendors of Windows devices provide a built-in recovery partition. This does consume a few gigabytes of storage space, and some users are tempted to liberate this space by deleting the partition. However, when you experience a serious startup problem, or some other issue that impairs the behaviour of Windows, you'll be glad you didn't delete it yourself.

Restoring Windows by using the vendor recovery partition wipes the device back to its out-of-the-box state and may result in complete data loss, depending on where your files are stored. If you sync your settings and data to OneDrive, then when you have completed the recovery process, you can sign in using your Microsoft account and sync your settings to the restored device.

To access the recovery partition, the procedure will vary according to your device type and the vendor who supplied it. In the case of my Lenovo tablet, pressing and holding the up volume and power buttons together brings up the tablet's startup recovery screen, from which I can choose to recover. You must consult your vendor's device documentation for specific information on your device.

Congratulations

This is the end of the book

I hope you enjoyed reading this book, and more importantly, that you found it useful. I shall continue to update the book on the Kindle store, so be sure to sync your copy on your reading device.

Andrew Warren

Congratulations - This is the end of the book

This page left intentionally blank

Printed in Great Britain
by Amazon.co.uk, Ltd.,
Marston Gate.